Literature

WHAT EVERY CATHOLIC SHOULD KNOW

Literature

WHAT EVERY CATHOLIC SHOULD KNOW

Joseph Pearce

IGNATIUS PRESS
San Francisco

AUGUSTINE INSTITUTE
Greenwood Village, CO

Ignatius Press
San Francisco, CA

Augustine Institute
Greenwood Village, CO

Cover Design: Ben Dybas

©2019 Ignatius Press, San Francisco,
and the Augustine Institute, Greenwood Village, CO
ISBN 978-1-7335221-2-0 (pbk)
ISBN 978-1-7338598-1-3 (hbk)
Library of Congress Control Number 2019934543

Printed in Canada ∞

For Dena Hunt, in admiration

Contents

1

Why Should Every Catholic Know About Literature?

There is a very good reason for every Catholic to know the great works of literature—and that is because the great works of literature help us to know ourselves. This is the reason that we should learn the humanities—because the humanities teach us about humanity, both our own humanity and the humanity of our neighbours.

In the great works of literature we discover a deep understanding of man's being and purpose. We discover that the human person is *homo viator*, a pilgrim or wayfarer who journeys through mortal life with eternal life always in mind. This understanding of who we are has been lost. "The modern man," wrote Chesterton, "is more like a traveller who has forgotten the name of his destination, and has to go back whence he came, even to find out where he is going." In fact, things are even worse than Chesterton imagined because modern man has not only forgotten the name of his destination, he has even forgotten that he has a destination. He does not know that he is a traveller. He is unaware that he is on a journey or that he has anywhere to go. He is not *homo viator*, but *homo superbus*, proud-man, a pathetic creature trapped within the confines of his own self-constructed "self," a prisoner of his own pride and prejudice.

The great works of literature show us the folly of *homo superbus* as well as the wisdom of *homo viator* by contrasting the viciousness of the prideful villain with the virtuous humility and humanity of the noble hero. They show us that the good man is inspired in all that he does by the desire to serve his God and his neighbour, while the bad man is inspired by his desire to please himself. They show us that man is always oscillating between the two poles of his very nature. He is either falling into the folly of the idolatrous love of himself above all others, or he is edified by his selfless love for the other. Since this oscillation between sin and virtue is to be found in the heart of every man, it is also to be found at the heart of every age in history and in all the great works written throughout every age in history.

Viewing the panoramic vista of the history of the West, we can see three broad ages of man. The first of these ages is the pre-Christian or pagan age; the second age is the age of Christendom; and the third age may be called the age of Disenchantment.

In the pre-Christian or pagan age, the artists and philosophers examined the struggle between *homo viator* and *homo superbus*, perceiving the superiority of the former over the latter, albeit through a glass darkly.

In the age of Christendom we see, subsumed within the very fibre of the individual's conscience and in the very fabric of human society, the affirmation of *homo viator* and the condemnation of *homo superbus*. Christendom's chief characteristic is its overarching unity in the realms of philosophy and theology, a unity in which *homo viator* is not only admired but enshrined. In Christendom, sanctity and heroism are synonymous, with the absence of the one invariably leading to the destruction of the other. And since, for the orthodox Christian, sanctity is also synonymous with sanity, it was incumbent upon all men to overcome the temptations of *homo superbus* (the barbarian within ourselves) and to become perfect examples of *homo viator* (the saint as the epitome of the civilised man). In this sense the age of Christendom corresponds to the finest flowering of civilisation. It is an age in which becoming civilised is the very goal of man's existence because being civilised (holy) is the only means of attaining the perfect civilisation of Heaven. It is, therefore, hardly surprising that the heart of Christendom—its theology, its philosophy, its painting, its architecture, its sculpture, its music, its literature—is the very incarnation of the integrated harmony, the wholeness and oneness, of its Founder.

In the age of Disenchantment, the wholeness and oneness of Christendom is lost in a progressive fragmentation of thought that continues to this day. From its earliest manifestation in the decay of the Christian humanism and neo-classicism of the Renaissance and its coming of age in the pride of the superciliously self-named Enlightenment, to its self-defeating victory in the nihilistic nonsense of deconstructionism, the age of Disenchantment represents the triumph of *homo superbus* over *homo viator* and, therefore, the triumph of barbarism over civilisation.

At this juncture, we should remind ourselves that these three ages do not represent a linear progression in the "right" direction, as the denizens of the age of Disenchantment would have us believe, but a manifestation of the perennial struggle between *homo superbus* and *homo viator*, between barbarism and civilisation. On the assumption that civilisation is preferable or superior to barbarism, it could be said more truthfully that the age of Disenchantment represents a move in a wrong or regressive direction. In any event, it is certainly wrong to presume that Disenchantment has replaced Christendom, in the sense that it has somehow eclipsed or extinguished the age that preceded it. On the contrary, Christendom is alive and well and existing simultaneously with Disenchantment. This should not surprise us because *homo superbus* can never utterly or ultimately defeat *homo viator*.

Although the culture has become fragmented and disintegrated in the age of Disenchantment, the presence of Christendom within the age of Disenchantment can be seen in the magic or miracle of Re-enchantment. Many of the greatest works of art in recent centuries are not the products of disenchantment but of re-enchantment. The works of Shakespeare, Dryden, Coleridge, Wordsworth, Dickens, Dostoyevsky, Chesterton, Lewis, Tolkien, Waugh, and Eliot, to name but an illustrious few, are inspired by a rejection of disenchantment and a desire for re-enchantment. And what is true of literature is true of painting (the Pre-Raphaelites), architecture (the Gothic Revival), and music (Bruckner, Mahler, Mendelssohn, Messiaen, Arvo Pärt, and others). This disillusionment with disenchantment represents a refusal to believe that reality is only the cold mechanism of the materialist or the meaningless mess of the nihilist; it is an awakening to the enchantment of reality, perceiving it as a miraculous harmony of being, a song, a Great Music, the Music of the Spheres. Hence the employment of "disenchantment" as the operative description of the process that calls itself the Enlightenment. The word *enchantment* derives from the Latin *cantare*, to sing, or *cantus*, song, and the disenchantment of the Enlightenment was the shift from seeing nature as creation, that is, as a beautiful work of art *sung* into existence by God, to nature as something merely mechanical and, later, as something merely meaningless. Thus, in the age of Disenchantment in which we currently find ourselves, the struggle between *homo superbus* and *homo viator* manifests itself in disenchantment and re-enchantment.

The great works of literature are works of enchantment which have the power to re-enchant the most weary of souls. They are the inheritance of all of us, or all of us who want them. In reading these great works we find ourselves in the presence of great minds thinking about great things. We find ourselves in the presence of almost three thousand years of genius. We find ourselves in the company of the *illustrissimi* of civilisation. In what better company could we possibly hope to spend our time? This side of the grave, there is no better company apart from the saints themselves. The better company, the best possible company, awaits *homo viator* after his temporal journey is over. In the meantime, and especially in the mean times in which we live, these great works of literature are good companions for the journey and excellent guides. Like the *lembas* which sustained Frodo and Sam on their journey through Mordor to Mount Doom in *The Lord of the Rings*, great literature is manna for the mind and food for the soul.

2

The Virgin Muse I:
The Epics of Homer and Virgil

Having discussed the importance of the great works of literature, and why, as Catholics, we should read them, let us continue by taking a voyage through the history of Western Civilisation, pausing along the way to look at those books we should especially get to know better.

Seeing the broad sweep of history in Christian terms, we can see the cultural tradition of Christendom as the fruits of the marriage between Christ and his Church. Prior to the coming of Christ, the Bridegroom, we can see the marriage being prepared in the theology and history of the Jews, and in the philosophy and literature of the Greeks. In the Old Covenant of the people of Israel, in the moral and metaphysical musings of the Greek poets, and in the love of wisdom of the sages of Athens, we see the preparation of a virgin culture for the wedding feast. With the coming of Christ, the Bride becomes one flesh with the Bridegroom, united in his Mystical Body. Thereafter, the fruits of genuine culture can be seen as the children of that mystical marriage.

The saints are of course children of that marriage but so, too, are the great works of civilisation. Even as the New Testament baptizes the Old Testament, so Boethius and Augustine baptize Plato, and Thomas Aquinas baptizes Aristotle. Dante baptizes Homer and Virgil, and Shakespeare baptizes Sophocles. This is the tree of cultural tradition, the family tree descending genealogically from the marriage of Christ and his Church.

At this point we might hear a dissident and dissonant voice, crying in the wilderness or the wasteland, claiming that we have forgotten those great works which are not Catholic or perhaps not even Christian. Are we suggesting that such works do not possess any cultural worth? This voice, which is the devil's or at least one of his advocates, does not know whence the springs of cultural life have their source. Any work of culture which shines forth the goodness, truth, and beauty of Triune reality is shining forth the truth of Christ and his Church, even if its author is unaware of the fact. Thus the works of Homer and Virgil prefigure Christian literature insofar as they are asking the right questions and coming to at least some of the right answers in their engagement with the great moral and metaphysical questions. Such works express the desire of the virgin for the coming of the Bridegroom.

Pre-Christian paganism grew in wisdom and maturity until she was ripe for the coming of the Bridegroom, whom she embraced with zeal. In contrast, "post-Christian" paganism has grown tired and weary of the responsibilities and sacrifices that her marriage to the Bridegroom demands, preferring to desert her Spouse and abandon the family in pursuit of a life of lechery in the desert of her just deserts. Whereas the pre-Christian pagans took the virgin path to the Bridegroom inherent in the wisdom and innocence of the quest for goodness, truth, and beauty, the "post-Christian" pagans can only return to the Bridegroom by the tried and tested path of the prodigal bride who, having wrecked herself on the rocks of her own recklessness, finally creeps home on the thorny path of contrition and penance.

The paganism which is worthy of respect has nothing to do with the divorcée, whose follies are worthy of pity, but with the virgin who awaits the coming of the Bridegroom. It is this pre-Christian or classical paganism that we celebrate.

And there is certainly much to celebrate.

Classical paganism brought forth the golden age of philosophy in which giants, such as Socrates, Plato, and Aristotle, mused upon the meaning of the cosmos and the meaning of life within it. This pagan philosophy, once quickened by the truths revealed by the Bridegroom, brought forth a new generation of Christian philosophy, her children including such giants as St. Augustine and St. Thomas Aquinas.

In a similar way, the great works of pagan literature also mused upon the meaning of the cosmos and the meaning of life within it, laying the very foundations for all the great literature that would follow in its wake. Let us take a closer look at this classical legacy that we have all inherited.

HOMER

Commencing our odyssey through the ages in the pre-Christian or pagan age, we can declare that Homer deserves a place among the truly great for the brilliance of his depiction of the goodness of *homo viator* and the follies of *homo superbus*. Indeed, one scarcely knows where to start in praising Homer, whose creative brilliance is unsurpassed in the whole history of human letters, with the possible and arguable exception of Dante and Shakespeare. His first epic, *The Iliad*, is a mystical meditation on the harmful consequences of man's folly and on the providential triumph of the will of God.

The Iliad

Sing, Muse, of Achilles's anger and its devastation . . . and of the will of Zeus which was done.

The opening lines of Homer's epic, *The Iliad*, say it all. In these first few words, the poet betrays his purpose and unpacks the deepest meaning of his work. His theme is the anger of Achilles and its destructive ramifications and how, in spite of Achilles's best-laid schemes, the will of Zeus is accomplished.

As for Zeus himself, there are inklings in *The Iliad* of his possessing the divine attributes of omniscience and omnipotence, suggesting that Homer's polytheism is moving inexorably towards monotheism. If, for instance, one God is more powerful than the combined power of all the other gods, it is not a great leap to see the other "gods" as being more like angels, lesser supernatural beings, good and bad, angelic and demonic, whose actions might bring discord but cannot ultimately alter the will of Almighty God. This suggestive parallel between the "gods" of Homer's paganism and the angels and demons of Christian theology is explored with unsurpassed brilliance in the mythopoeic world of J. R. R. Tolkien.

Nor should we forget that Homer begins his epic with a prayer to his Muse, the goddess of creativity, requesting the grace he needs to tell the story well and honestly. In doing so, he is acknowledging that creativity is a gift of the gods and that without their supernatural help (grace) the Poet or Artist can achieve nothing. His work is therefore a work of piety, as well as a work of poetry. He desires to tell the truth and seeks the help of divine intercession to enable him to do so.

The truth he intends to tell is not factual or historical truth because he is writing of the stuff of legend and of events that happened several centuries earlier. He will, therefore, tell his tale using the poetic license necessary to tell a good story, weaving fact with fiction into a seamless narrative fabric. No, the truth he means to tell is not historical truth (facts), but *moral* truth. He is going to present to us, in powerful dramatic form, an important moral lesson, holding up the "mirror to man" which, as Tolkien suggests, is one of the main purposes of myth or fairy stories. The moral he is going to present is that anger, the cankered fruit of pride, is destructive and that it has devastating consequences, not merely for Achilles, the prideful man, full of wrath, but for countless other people, the innocent victims of Achilles's sin. Thus, in Robert Fitzgerald's translation, Achilles's "doomed and ruinous" anger "caused the Akhaians loss on bitter loss and crowded brave souls into the undergloom, leaving so many dead men—carrion for dogs and birds." Sin does not merely harm the sinner but countless others also. Actions have consequences and bad actions have bad consequences. This is Homer's lesson. It is, however, not his only lesson. We forget, at our peril, that this connection between immoral behaviour and destruction is not merely fatalistic but providential. It is, as Homer is at pains to point out, "the will of Zeus which was done."

As Achilles's rage runs riot, riding roughshod over his reason as much as it rides roughshod over his neighbours (both his friends and enemies), he incurs the wrath of God. In following his own prideful passion for revenge rather than the path of virtue, Achilles brings down the judgment of Zeus upon himself. His destruction is, therefore, not merely the workings of blind fate but of divine providence.

The pride of *homo superbus*, represented by the actions of Agamemnon and Paris, as well as those of Achilles, is duly punished in accordance with the overriding will of Zeus; it is, therefore, surely significant that the epic ends with praises being sung for the fallen and "blameless" hero, Hector, and not for his conqueror, Achilles. It might also be argued that Homer presents us with the key to understanding his own moral position in the metaphors of reconciliation offered in the epic's penultimate book, in which magnanimity and forgiveness triumph over prideful vengeance.

This understanding of *The Iliad* is in complete harmony with the insistence of Tolkien and C. S. Lewis that the pagan myths contain splintered fragments of the one true light that comes from God. For Tolkien and Lewis, the pagans were looking for the light that would eventually be revealed in Christ and were assisted in that quest by the grace of the God that they did not know. As Lewis tells us in *The Pilgrim's Regress*, God inspired the pagans with pictures (myths) because they had forgotten how to read (that is, they did not know the law or the prophets). Homer's Muse was, therefore, a grace that he only partially comprehended but which he served with the utmost fidelity, with triumphant results.

To be sure, Homer is not a Christian and the god he worships is not the Christian God. Yet he believes that his talents as a poet are God-given gifts, and he prays to the giver of the gifts for the grace to use them well. He then employs these gifts to show us that the sins of pride and anger are self-destructive, and destructive of others also, and that such sin will not go unpunished by a god who commands that men live virtuously. He is, therefore, a writer of the highest order that Christians and indeed all men of good will should feel comfortable calling a friend and ally.

The Odyssey

Oh for shame, how the mortals put the blame upon us gods, for they say evils come from us, but it is they, rather, who by their own recklessness win sorrow beyond what is given.

Homer's other great epic, *The Odyssey*, casts Odysseus as the archetypal *homo viator*, the man on a journey or quest who must grow in virtue in order to attain his "heavenly" reward. His journey home reflects the journey home on which all of us are embarked. Our life journey is indeed a journey, as our life story is indeed a story. It has a beginning, a middle, and an end, like all good journeys and all good stories. It has a purpose, which is to achieve the goal, ultimately to reach that place which we call home, that place where we belong, the place where we love and are loved. The place that our heart desires and towards which it strives.

Along the way, we will face challenges and setbacks. We will make mistakes, and, if we learn from them, we will make progress by not repeating them. We will learn that humility leads to wisdom and that pride precedes a fall. We will learn to respect both God and neighbour, which the Greeks enshrined in the law of *xenia*, the law which demands hospitality between host and guest and which demands respect for the stranger. We will learn, as Odysseus does, that the bigger we think we are the smaller we really are, and that the smaller we think we are the greater we become. We will learn that humility is not only the beginning of wisdom but the beginning of the way home. We will learn that the journey requires self-sacrifice, which is merely another word for love, the laying down of ourselves for others, and that, unless we make such sacrifices, no progress on the journey is possible.

At the heart of the epic is the problem of suffering, or the problem of pain, as C. S. Lewis called it in his book of that name, which has been one of the most difficult of all the conundrums with which philosophers and theologians have grappled throughout the ages of man.

Why does suffering happen? Does it have any purpose or meaning, or is it pointless and senseless? If God exists, is he to blame for all the suffering in the world? And if he is to blame, what sort of sadistic God rules the cosmos? And, since such a God would militate against everything the philosophers and theologians have taught about the perfection of God, would not the existence of suffering prove the non-existence of God?

These are great questions, which should not be shunned or shrugged off by those who have faith in the existence of God, or, for that matter, by those who have no faith in his existence. In short, the problem of pain is a challenge to our understanding of the cosmos, whether we are believers or non-believers, whether we are Christians or atheists.

Many great insights into the meaning of suffering can be found in the arts, especially in the art of literature, which complement the attempts of the philosophers and theologians to get to grips with this most axiomatic of problems. From the earliest days, the poets have grappled with the problem and have even suggested answers. Thus, the words of Zeus quoted above, as rendered in Richmond Lattimore's translation of *The Odyssey* (Book One, lines 32–34). Homer puts these words into the mouth of the Father of gods and men at the beginning of his epic not only to address the question of suffering but also to suggest an answer. It is not the gods who are to blame for suffering, says Zeus, but the recklessness, that is, the sinfulness, of men. Homer shows repeatedly that men are their own worst enemies, heaping suffering upon suffering upon themselves through their own selfish actions. We have seen that Achilles's anger in *The Iliad* is shown to be destructive to his friends as well as his enemies, and ultimately to himself. Paris's elopement with Helen launches the thousand ships that destroy Troy. The reckless disobedience of Odysseus's men leads to their destruction, as does the recklessness of the suitors besieging the beautiful Penelope in Ithaka.

Sin is self-destructive. In this sense Zeus is absolutely right. We have no right to blame the gods, or God, for our suffering if it has been caused by our own recklessness. We only have ourselves to blame.

But what about the innocent victims of the sins of others? What about the innocent victims of Achilles's anger and Paris's lust? What about the ordinary people of Troy? What about "blameless" Hector and his equally blameless wife and child? Why should *they* suffer? How are *they* to blame? Or, to put the whole question in the modern idiom, why do bad things happen to good people?

Perhaps Zeus might answer these questions with the retort that the gods are not to blame for the sins of men. In other words, if Hector and his wife and child are blameless, so are the gods. Blame Achilles and Paris for the destruction of their innocent victims, Zeus would retort, but do not blame me.

There is, however, a further question that arises from Zeus's defence of himself. If he is so powerful, why does he permit the innocent to suffer? Why should the sins of the guilty cause suffering to the guiltless? If God could prevent such suffering of the innocent victims of sin but refrains from doing so, is he not also to blame? Is he not in some way an accessory to the sin? In other words, how can a good God permit bad things to happen to good people?

There is a hint that Homer had asked these difficult questions insofar as Zeus states that the recklessness of mortals brings sorrow "beyond what is given." In other words, even without human recklessness, some suffering "is given." One thinks perhaps of earthquakes or other natural disasters. Why does God permit such things to happen? The answer is that they are "given" as a gift to bring us to our senses because the proud heart cannot love unless it is broken. "And I will give you a new heart," says the Lord, "and put a new spirit within you: and I will take away the stony heart out of your flesh, and will give you a heart of flesh" (Ez 36:26). "But God's eternal laws are kind," writes Oscar Wilde in *The Ballad of Reading Gaol*, "and break the heart of stone." And so broken hearts are necessary because, as Wilde asks, "how else but through a broken heart may Lord Christ enter in?"

Although Homer is not a Christian, he grapples heroically with the problem of suffering in *The Odyssey*, suggesting that Odysseus can only grow in wisdom and virtue if his pride is broken through the breaking of his heart. His return home is delayed by the gods until he is punished for his sins and until he has cleansed his soul of the pride which had caused his fall. In this sense Odysseus's journey can be seen as purgatorial.

As with the protagonists in *The Iliad*, Odysseus is punished when he forgets his calling as *homo viator* and succumbs instead to the temptation of *homo superbus*. His boastfulness after the blinding of Polyphemus brings down the curse that destroys his men and delays his own homecoming. If he had been content in decorous humility to remain "Nobody" he would have arrived home expeditiously with his men and ships unharmed; in succumbing to the pride of exalting himself, he is humbled by the punishment of the gods.

The Odyssey's subplot also revolves around the theme of man as *homo viator* in the growth to physical and emotional maturity of Telemachos. The journey of Odysseus's son from the inadequacy of boyhood to the fullness of manhood is *homo viator's* rite of passage. Finally, for good measure, Homer gives us in the figure of Penelope an icon of idealized femininity, a paragon of womanly virtue worthy of the company of Dante's Beatrice and Shakespeare's Cordelia and Portia, all of whom are a reflection, either via prefiguration or re-presentation, of the Marian archetype presented by what Tolkien would call the True Myth of Christianity.

In a true reading of the timeless myths of antiquity we do not find distance and dissonance between ourselves and our ancestors but resolution and resonance. We can be at home with Homer because Homer is as homely as we are. He points the way Home. He experiences the exile of life and desires the community and communion of Home, in its physical and its metaphysical sense. The only person who is not at home with Homer is the person who does not believe in Home, the person who believes that there is no such thing as Home, the person who believes that man is not an exiled soul yearning for home but a truly homeless waif who has no home to go to, the person who knows only John Lennon's Nowhere Man. Homer is not such a person. He knew better; so did Virgil, Dante, Chaucer, Shakespeare, and Tolkien. They knew the connection between Everyman and the Everlasting Man. The classical muse and the Christian muse are in harmony; it is only poor (post)modern man, cut off from his inheritance, who lives in discord, believing that he has no purpose and nowhere to go.

So, let us end our brief discussion of *The Odyssey* by returning to our original question and answering it definitively. What has Odysseus to do with us? The answer is that he has everything to do with us because he is who we are.

VIRGIL

The Aeneid

The other great pagan epic, written in Latin and not Greek, is *The Aeneid* by the Roman writer, Virgil. Although he wrote in a different language than Homer, and from a very different cultural perspective, and although he wrote almost seven hundred years later, he was greatly influenced by Homer's epics, without which his own epic would have been quite literally unimaginable.

Writing only about 25 years before the birth of Christ, Virgil's epic may be described as a sequel to *The Iliad* and *The Odyssey*. It is the story of Aeneas, one of the Trojan heroes in *The Iliad*. In Homer's epic, Aeneas fights Achilles in single combat and is a favourite of the god Poseidon who declares that it is Aeneas's destiny to escape the fall of Troy "to ensure that the great line of Dardanus may not unseeded perish from the world." Poseidon declares that it is the will of Zeus that "Aeneas and his sons, and theirs, will be lords over Trojans born hereafter" (Book Twenty, Fitzgerald translation). Reading this passage in *The Iliad*, Virgil was inspired to imagine Aeneas not merely as the survivor of the fall of Troy who is destined to rule the remnant of the Trojan people but as the very founder of Rome. This, therefore, is the imaginative seed, a gift from Homer, which would grow into Virgil's great epic.

Virgil's purpose, according to his translator, Robert Fitzgerald, was "to enfold in the mythical action of *The Aeneid* foreshadowings and direct foretellings of Roman history, more than a thousand years of it between Aeneas and his own time."[1] In order to achieve this, Virgil reverses the roles of the heroes and villains, making the Trojans the heroes and the Greeks the villains. Odysseus, for instance, is vilified, a negative portrayal which would lead to Dante placing the hero of *The Odyssey* in the Hell of his *Divine Comedy*. Dante, as a literary disciple of Virgil, sees things through Virgilian and not Homeric eyes, a fact that should be borne in mind when we read the *Inferno*.

The irony is that Virgil's patriotic epic, which serves as a poetic eulogy to the glory of Rome and its Empire, owes its form, its inspirational source, and its cultural roots to the very Greeks whom the Romans had conquered and whom Virgil vilifies. The Romans conquered the Greeks, writes Fitzgerald, "and were conquered in their turn by Greek literature, philosophy, and art. And they grew fond, no one quite knows why, of tracing their origin to the emigration of surviving Trojans under Aeneas."[2]

Perhaps the most memorable part of *The Aeneid* is the story, told in Book IV of the epic, of the passionately erotic and recklessly irresponsible relationship between Aeneas, future founder of Rome, and Dido, Queen of Carthage. This is surely one of the greatest tragic love stories ever told, rivalling that of Paris and Helen in *The Iliad*, of Paolo and Francesca in *The Divine Comedy*, and Romeo and Juliet in Shakespeare's play. Caught in the throes of their obsessive passion for each other, Aeneas and Dido neglect their duties as leaders of their respective peoples, sacrificing all stately responsibilities on the altar of erotic self-indulgence.

---

1   Virgil, *The Aeneid* (New York: Vintage Classics, 1990), 405.
2   Ibid.

In those days Rumor took an evil joy
At filling the countryside with whispers, whispers,
Gossip of what was done, and never done:
How this Aeneas landed, Trojan born,
How Dido in her beauty graced his company,
Then how they reveled all the winter long
Unmindful of the realm, prisoners of lust.[3]

Aeneas is finally brought to his senses after God (Jupiter) sends his messenger (Mercury) to command that Aeneas put his vocation, his calling, which is to found Rome, above illicit worldly pleasures.

As the sharp admonition and command
From heaven had shaken him awake, he now
Burned only to be gone, to leave that land
Of the sweet life behind.[4]

Aeneas tries to explain to Queen Dido why he has no choice, under the circumstances, but to leave her and to do his duty, obeying thereby the demands of his calling and the commands of God. He had been haunted in his dreams by his father's troubled ghost; he had feelings of guilt that he was betraying his son of his promised inheritance, "[m]y dear boy wronged, defrauded of his kingdom"; and then he had been visited by an angelic messenger from God himself admonishing him to do as his destiny demanded. "So please," he tells the anguished Queen, "no more of these appeals that set us both afire. I sail for Italy not of my own free will." It is not that he literally has no free will; he is not an automaton; it is that the demands of his conscience and his responsibilities to both God and family take precedence over his personal feelings or passions. As a good man, doing what he should

---

3   Ibid., 102.
4   Ibid., 105.

and not what he could, he chooses the better path, which is the path of self-sacrifice.

Duty-bound

Aeneas, though he struggled with desire
To calm and comfort her in all her pain,
To speak to her and turn her mind from grief,
And though he sighed his heart out, shaken still
With love of her, yet took the course heaven gave him
And went back to the fleet.[5]

Her love turned to hatred, Dido chooses an altogether different form of self-sacrifice to that chosen by Aeneas. Abandoning reason and her own responsibilities to her people, she decides in a fit of deadly madness to end her misery by committing suicide.

So broken in mind by suffering, Dido caught
Her fatal madness and resolved to die.[6]

There is much more in *The Aeneid* that warrants our attention, apart from this timelessly powerful and perennially relevant human tragedy, but time and space demand that we move to literary pastures new, turning our attention from epic poetry to tragic drama.

5　Ibid., 110.
6　Ibid., 113.

3

The Virgin Muse II:
The Tragic Drama of Sophocles

It is important to remember that the great pre-Christian writers were pagans and not relativists. As such, they knew that truth not only exists but that it transcends physical reality. This is why they give us blind seers such as Teiresias or Oedipus who see with the eyes of wisdom and faith even though they cannot see the purely physical things around them. Homer and Sophocles knew that Teiresias and Oedipus see better than worldly cynics because they see the *truth*. Relativists, on the other hand, are blinded by their faith in themselves. They are neither theists nor polytheists but simply old-fashioned idolaters, idolizing themselves as the arbiters and touchstone of the "truth" that is mere opinion.

In Aeschylus's *Oresteia* and Sophocles's *Oedipus Cycle*, we see the first buds of a new springtime of philosophical questioning prophesying the full flowering of Greek philosophy under Socrates, Plato, and Aristotle. Aeschylus asks fundamental questions about the nature of justice and the role of the divine in breaking the endless cycle of vengeance inherent in human law; Sophocles shows us Oedipus as a Job-like figure, more sinned against than sinning, who grows in wisdom and virtue through the experience of suffering until, ripened into sanctity, he warrants a mystical assumption into Heaven at the end of his life.

The three Theban plays by Sophocles, known collectively as *The Oedipus Cycle*, compete in brilliance with the great dramatic masterpieces of Shakespeare. From the cautionary political philosophy of *Antigone* to the mystical assumption of Oedipus into Heaven, the three Theban plays prefigure the Christian truths to which they point. In *Antigone*, Sophocles gives us a perennially relevant work of literature, providing profound insights into the relationship between religion and the state, and between natural law and human law. Antigone's adherence to the rights of religion over those of the state, and her insistence that the natural law cannot be contradicted by human law, is rooted in her understanding of herself as a creature owing obedience and service to the Creator.

Unfortunately, in spite of their perennial applicability to all ages, the modern world misreads the plays of Sophocles as it misreads those of Shakespeare.

Take the character of Oedipus, for instance.

Poor old Oedipus. Not only was he the victim of circumstances beyond his ken and control, he has been tainted in our own deplorable epoch by having a Freudian "complex" named after him. For those blessed enough to be ignorant of the notion of the Oedipus Complex, as was everyone prior to Freud's "discovery" of it at the end of the nineteenth century, it is a child's unconscious and neurotic sexual desire for its opposite-sex parent, usually a boy's sexual desire for his mother. The irony is that Oedipus cannot possibly have suffered from the "complex" that Freud unjustly pinned on him. As a boy he did not even know his own mother, and therefore could not possibly have had sexual designs upon her, unconsciously or otherwise. As an adult he falls in love and marries a woman, blissfully ignorant of the fact that she is his biological mother. When he discovers the awful truth, he blinds himself in an apoplectic fit of penitential rage and self-loathing. All of this is told by Sophocles in his play *Oedipus Rex* and, as Sophocles shows us in the play's sequel, *Oedipus at Colonus*, the experience of being the victim of circumstances of which he was entirely ignorant and therefore entirely innocent leads to a growth in wisdom, fortified by the knowledge that, like Shakespeare's Lear, he has been more sinned against than sinning. Ultimately his attainment of the wisdom that comes from the acceptance of suffering leads to his being taken up into Heaven by the gods.

Sophocles's noble paganism, which prefigures the redemptive suffering at the heart of Christianity, is sullied and soiled by the smutty imagination of the sex-obsessed Freud, who has made of Oedipus a byword for a perversion of which the tragic hero was clearly not guilty. This would have been bad enough; yet Freud went even further in his defamation of virtuous characters in literature, dragging the noble Hamlet through the same ignoble mire through which he had dragged the hapless Oedipus. In his morally iconoclastic book, *The Interpretation of Dreams* (1899), Freud claimed that the play *Hamlet* "has its roots in the same soil as *Oedipus Rex*": "In [*Oedipus Rex*] the child's wishful fantasy that underlies it is brought into the open and realized as it would be in a dream. In *Hamlet* it remains repressed; and—just as in the case of a neurosis—we only learn of its existence from its inhibiting consequences." Anyone who knows either play should be astonished at Freud's woeful misreading of each of these thoroughly moral texts, the one prefiguring Christian morality and the other manifesting it. And yet the blind Oedipus, like the blind Tiresias before him and the blind Gloucester after him, sees more than Freud and those wilfully self-blinded souls who follow in Freud's eros-blinded and venereal footsteps. "I stumbled when I saw," says Gloucester in *King Lear*, his words serving as a warning to those who refuse to see the light of day because they prefer the darkness of the night. Such is the case with the way that Greek or Shakespearean tragedies are so often produced in our darkened days.

Let us conclude our discussion of pre-Christian literature with a summary of its legacy.

The fundamental questions asked by the giants of Greek literature were taken up by the great Greek philosophers, and it has been said that all subsequent philosophy is but footnotes on the ideas enunciated by the Greeks. It is indeed one of the great tragedies of the age of Disenchantment that the footnotes to Plato and Aristotle are being written by those who have not understood the text upon which they are commenting. For the age of Christendom, however, the Greeks were allies upon whom the foundations of Christian philosophy were laid. Augustine, Thomas Aquinas, and the great Christian philosophers were greatly indebted to Plato and Aristotle and used the ideas of their illustrious forebears to forge the impregnable armour of *fides et ratio* (faith and reason) with which Christendom has withstood the claims of heretical theology and false philosophy.

The Great Books of early Christendom, such as Augustine's *Confessions* and *City of God* and Boethius's *Consolation of Philosophy*, bear the hallmark of Greek philosophy, and the highest philosophical achievement of the whole of Christendom, the *Summa* of Thomas Aquinas, can be seen as a dialogue with, and a perfection of, Aristotelianism. Dante's *Divine Comedy*, Christendom's highest work of literary art, which is a poetic commentary on Aquinas's *Summa*, was greatly inspired aesthetically by Virgil, who was himself inspired by Homer.

In addition, this classical muse can also be seen wending its way to Canterbury with Chaucer's pilgrims and flitting through the plays of Shakespeare. And yet the muse that inspired Chaucer's *Knight's Tale* or Shakespeare's *Pericles* was not truly classical; it was truly Christian. The truly classical muse is only to be found in unbaptized antiquity. It has its fulfilment and consummation in Christ and ceases to exist following the Incarnation. It is consumed by its consummation.

Through his Incarnation, and his Death and Resurrection, Christ consummates his love for humanity, vitalizing culture with his Presence. He is the fulfilment of the Old Law of the Jews, but he is also the fulfilment of the twilit gropings of the Gentiles. He is the consummation of the pre-Christian musings of Homer, Aeschylus, Sophocles, and Virgil, and is the fulfilment of their honest, artistic articulation of moral truths and precepts; he is the consummation of the rationally articulate but visually impaired philosophical musings of Socrates, Plato, and Aristotle. He baptizes their desire and pours forth the fullness of the Truth that was beyond their grasp. He is the Way, the Truth, and the Life for which they were seeking. He is also the End of their search, in both senses of the word, and is, therefore, the end of them. Henceforth the virgin musings of the pagans are no longer possible because the pagan imagination has lost its virginity. Renewed and reborn in Christ through his Mystical Marriage with his Bride (the Church), the Muse becomes graceful in the literal sense in which it is filled with grace.

4

Early Christian Literature:
From Boethius to Beowulf

In the Gospels, we are shown the deepest truths by means of a narrative. God reveals himself to us by telling us a story about himself, and he reveals ourselves in relation to him by means of the same story. He does not show us merely abstract concepts, in the manner of Euclid; he shows himself to us in the unfolding of his story (history) and in the recording of this story in his book (the Bible). His own Life, Death, and Resurrection has quite rightly been called "the greatest story ever told," as it was also, of course, the greatest story ever lived. Christ can be seen to be teaching us through the facts of his life as he lives it, but also, and crucially, in the stories he tells us through the means of his parables, the stories within the Story. These parables are fictional narratives, the figments of Our Lord's imagination, containing characters who never lived in history except as characters in a story. The Prodigal Son is not a real-life historical character who really lived in time but a fictional character in a make-believe story who teaches us priceless lessons about who we are as sons and daughters of God. In some sense, the Prodigal Son is more real, or at least more powerful, than any real-life character could ever be. He stands as a type, an archetype, an Everyman figure who shows men and women from all generations who they are in relation to God and their neighbour.

What God has done in the telling of his story in history and in the telling of fictional stories in his parables is sanctify story itself. Storytelling is God's chosen method of telling the truth. This being so, we can see how our own stories, in their own small way, can also be conveyers of truth, and we can see how the Christian era has breathed new life into literature by sanctifying the role of storytelling.

All of this goes to show that we are meant by the Storyteller himself to see the truth in stories and, therefore, by extension, that we are meant to imitate Christ in telling the truth through the telling of stories. We are meant to do so because we are ourselves in a story, or, rather, *the* story, his story. To tell stories is merely to tell things as they are. We are not merely *Anthropos*, which in Greek means "he who looks up"—in wonder (at the stars, for instance); we are also, as we keep reiterating, *homo viator*, man on a journey, the journey of life, with the soul's sole purpose of getting to Heaven. This means that each of our lives should be seen as a quest or a pilgrimage, which can only be understood in terms of a narrative. Our life-journey is a life-story.

The way in which we see the truth in the story depends on our ability to see the allegory or symbols that are present in the stories.

Allegory comes in many shapes and sizes so it is important that we know what it is and how we can distinguish between its various forms. The word *allegory* derives from the Greek word *allegoria*, which is itself the combination of two other Greek words: *allos*, meaning "other," and *agoria*, meaning "speaking." At its most basic level, allegory is, therefore, any thing which "speaks" or points to another thing. In this sense, as Saint Augustine states in *De doctrina Christiana* (*On Christian Doctrine*), every word is an allegory, a conventional sign that signifies something else. The word *dog* is a sound, when spoken, or a series of three shapes (letters) arranged in a certain order, when written, which signifies a four-legged canine mammal. Each of the three letters arranged in the certain order to make the word *dog* are themselves allegories, signifying certain sounds. If we were to shuffle those three allegorical signifiers into the reverse order it would make a word which signifies something very different from a dog: *god*. Letters and words are the most basic forms of allegory, things that speak of other things, but there are many other types of allegory. The parables of Christ are allegories in that they are one kind of thing, fictional stories, that speaks of another thing, namely, the moral lesson to be learned as being applicable to our own lives and the lives of our neighbours. Insofar as the Prodigal Son, or his forgiving father, or his envious brother remind us of ourselves or others, they are allegorical figures.

There is another simpler form of allegory in which characters are reduced to being mere personified abstractions, which is to say that they only exist to represent an abstract concept. Examples of this form of allegorical figure would be the Lady Philosophy in Boethius's *Consolation of Philosophy*, or the Giant Despair in Bunyan's *Pilgrim's Progress*, or the Lady Reason with her younger sisters Philosophy and Theology in C. S. Lewis's *Pilgrim's Regress*. This form of allegory was described by C. S. Lewis in his book *The Allegory of Love*:

> On the one hand you can start with an immaterial fact, such as the passions which you actually experience, and can then invent visibilia (visible things) to express them. If you are hesitating between an angry retort and a soft answer, you can express your state of mind by inventing a person called Ira (anger) with a torch and letting her contend with another invented person called Patientia (patience). This is allegory.[1]

---

1   As quoted in Walter Hooper, *C. S. Lewis: A Companion & Guide* (New York: Harper Collins, 1997), 551.

The problem is that this is not allegory *per se* but only a particular type of allegory, the sort of allegory which employs personified abstractions. It is not allegory in the broad sense in which every word is an allegory, or in the sense that the moral implicit in a parable can be said to be allegorical. This failure of Lewis to distinguish between the various forms of allegory has caused a great deal of confusion, especially when Lewis goes to great pains to insist that the Chronicles of Narnia are not allegories. It is true that the Narnia books are not allegories in the formal sense which Lewis describes in *The Allegory of Love*. Aslan reminds us of Christ, but he is not a personified abstraction, as is the Lady Philosophy in Boethius. It is in this sense that Lewis means that the Narnia stories are not allegories, and, in this sense, he is of course correct.

We can see, therefore, that one of the earliest Christian writers, Saint Augustine, building on ideas to be found in Plato, shows us the way that we should read literature. Meanwhile, another early Christian writer, Boethius, exemplified the form of literature, known as formal allegory, in which abstract ideas are personified as characters in a story.

Let us turn now to the earliest literature in the English language. Probably dating from the early eighth century, making it contemporaneous with the lives of Saints Boniface and Bede, *Beowulf* is a narrative animated by the rich Christian spirit of the culture from which it sprang, brimming over with allegorical potency and evangelical zeal. It also conveys a deep awareness of classical antiquity, drawing deep inspirational draughts from Virgil's *Aeneid*, highlighting the Saxon poet's awareness of his place within an unbroken cultural continuum. *Beowulf* is itself arguably the most important literary influence on *The Lord of the Rings*, exemplifying how this Anglo-Saxon epic is itself a part of that same priceless continuum, the inheritance that we call Christian civilisation.

Beowulf is divided into three sections in which the eponymous hero fights three different monsters. In the first two episodes, as Beowulf confronts and ultimately defeats Grendel and then Grendel's mother, the work is primarily a narrative in which the theological dimension is subsumed parabolically, especially in the recurring motif that human will and strength are insufficient, in the absence of divine assistance, to defeat the power of evil. This is presumably an orthodox riposte to the heresy of Pelagianism,[2] which plagued Saxon England and which is a major preoccupation of Bede in his *Ecclesiastical History*, probably written at around the same time as *Beowulf*.[3] *The Lord of the Rings* adopts a very similar approach in the way that it subsumes the presence of grace within the fabric of the story, unobtrusively and yet inescapably, something which is beyond the scope of our present discussion. It is, however, the allegorical technique that the *Beowulf* poet employs in the final section of the epic which most illumines the technique that Tolkien will himself employ in his own epic, emulating the anonymous poet who had taught him more than anyone else about the art of storytelling.

The dragon section of *Beowulf* commences with the theft of "a gem-studded goblet"[4] from the dragon's hoard, an act which gained the thief nothing but which provoked the destructive wrath of the dragon. Beowulf takes eleven comrades with him as he goes to meet the dragon in combat, plus the thief, "the one who had started all this strife" and who "was now added

---

2   The Pelagians believed that men could forge their own eternal destiny, earning themselves a place in Heaven by obeying the teachings of Christ through a triumph of the human will over temptation. Such a belief denied the need for grace and therefore denied the need for the Church and her sacraments.

3   There is much disagreement about the exact dating of *Beowulf*, its composition being shrouded in mystery. The present author agrees with those, including Tolkien, who believe it was written sometime between the mid-seventh and mid-eighth century.

4   All quotations from *Beowulf* are from Seamus Heaney's translation (New York: W. W. Norton & Company, 2002).

as a thirteenth to their number." Unlike the eleven who had accompanied their lord willingly, the thief was "press-ganged and compelled" to go with them, acting as their unwilling guide to the dragon's den. Clearly the *Beowulf* poet is employing numerical signification to draw parallels between Beowulf's fight to the death with the dragon (an iconic signification of the devil) and Christ's own fight to the death with the power of evil in his Passion. Equally clearly, *Beowulf* is not a formal or simple allegory because no character in the epic is merely a personified abstraction. Beowulf is not literally Christ, though he could be called a figure of Christ, one who is meant to remind us of Christ; the dragon is not literally Satan, though he or it is evidently intended to remind us of the devil himself. Similarly, the thief is not Judas (nor Adam) but is intended to remind us of the disciple whose act of treachery brought about his lord's death, and the other eleven are of course reminiscent of the other eleven apostles. The numerical coincidence exhibits the poet's intention of drawing parallels between his own story and its biblical parallel without ever succumbing to the level of formal allegory. Beowulf is always Beowulf, even though he is meant to remind us of Christ.

Continuing the allusive parallels, this time with Christ's agony in the Garden, we are told that, on the eve of battle, Beowulf is "sad at heart, unsettled yet ready, sensing his death." Later, as battle is about to commence, Beowulf's appointed followers, "that hand-picked troop," "broke ranks and ran for their lives," all except one, Wiglaf, who emerges as the signifier of St. John, the only one of Christ's apostles who remained at his side during the Crucifixion. Wiglaf reprimands his comrades for their cowardice in deserting their lord, reminding them that Beowulf had "picked us out from the army deliberately, honored us and judged us fit for this action."

Prior to his death, Beowulf instructs Wiglaf to order his men to build a burial mound in remembrance of him. After his death, ten shamefaced warriors emerge from the woods, indicating that the thief was not among them. At the poem's conclusion there are once again twelve warriors riding ceremoniously around the burial mound, which had been duly constructed in accordance with Beowulf's command, indicating that the traitor had been replaced by a new member, reminiscent of the appointment of St. Matthias to replace Judas as the twelfth apostle.

Although nobody would suggest that *Beowulf* is an allegory in the formal or crude sense, it is clear that the poet intends his audience to see suggestive parallels between Beowulf's sacrifice of himself in the battle against evil and that of the archetypal sacrifice of God himself on Calvary. For the Christian—and the *Beowulf* poet was indubitably Christian—all acts of genuine love involve the laying down of our lives for another. Furthermore, all those who genuinely love in this way are figures of Christ, from whom all genuine love flows and towards whom all genuine love points. In true life as in true literature all those who live and love like Christ are Christ-like and, as such, can be said to be figures of Christ. Christ is the *archetype* of which all virtuous men, in fact and in fiction, are *types*. The *Beowulf* poet shows this through the use of numerical clues. Tolkien does something very similar in his own work, emulating the work of his Anglo-Saxon mentor.

Although *Beowulf* is the best-known poem in Old English it is by no means the only poetic jewel in the Anglo-Saxon crown. "The Ruin," "The Wanderer," "The Seafarer," and "The Dream of the Rood" have each strode across the continuum of the centuries with the consummate ease that is the mark of all great art. The timely and timeless reminders of man's mortality are almost ubiquitous in these poems, palpitating like the heartbeat at the poetic core of life itself. Take, for instance, this wonderful evocation of deceased forebears from "The Ruin":

> Earthgrip holds them—gone, long gone, fast in gravesgrasp . . .
> . . . sank to loam-crust.[5]

Yet if the Anglo-Saxons were close to death, they were also close to life, in the sense that they were truly alive. They were close to nature, living off the fruits of the loam-crust until in the fullness of time sinking into it. Thus the imagery is primal, dealing with the primal realities of man's dependence on nature. Hail, falling on "the frost-bound earth," is described as the "coldest of grains." Fishermen are the ploughmen of the sea, who "drive the foam-furrow" to harvest the sea's fruit. The Seafarer is close to the creatures of the earth, with whom he shares an intimate communion, invoking his knowledge of birds and beasts to incant potent images of the "clinging sorrow" of his "breast-drought" . . .

> . . . for men's laughter
> there was curlew-call, there were cries of gannets,
> for mead-drinking the music of the gull . . .
>
> And the cuckoo calls him in his care-laden voice,
> scout of summer, sings of new griefs
> that shall make breast-hoard bitter
>
> Cuckoo's dirge drags out my heart,
> whets will to the whale's beat
> across wastes of water: far warmer to me
> are the Lord's kindnesses than this life of death
> lent us on land.

How much more alive were these Anglo-Saxons than are we moderns! They lived in a world that was harsh and hard, but at least it was real. We live in our computer-generated demi-worlds, centred on ourselves, utterly addicted to the

---

5   All the Anglo-Saxon poems quoted in the remainder of this chapter are Michael Alexander's translations as published in *The Earliest English Poems* (London: Penguin Books, 1966).

artificial-life support machine which drips the anodyne into the anoesis of our comfortably numb minds. How can we experience the beauty of this Old English poetry if we have never heard a curlew, or a gannet, or a cuckoo, or a gull? How can we experience Keats if we have never heard a nightingale, or Shelley if we have never heard a skylark?

And what is true of the natural is equally true of the supernatural. Unlike us moderns, the Anglo-Saxons were closely connected with the supernatural realities underpinning human existence. They called these realities "wyrd," a word which has decayed into the much weaker "weird." *Wyrd* was more than merely weird. It was the intimate, almost palpable, presence of Providence in the lives of men, the closeness and connectedness of God to the destiny of his creatures.

> Who liveth alone longeth for mercy,
> Maker's mercy. Though he must traverse
> Tracts of sea, sick at heart,
> Trouble with oars ice-cold waters,
> The ways of exile—Wyrd is set fast . . .
>
> In the earth-realm all is crossed;
> Wyrd's will changeth the world.
> Wealth is lent us, friends are lent us,
> Man is lent us, kin is lent;
> All this earth's frame shall stand empty

For the modern in his electronic dream-world this is but foolishness. He has no concept of wyrd. For him the wyrd is just weird, or, worse, merely absurd. Our ancestors' closeness to the natural and the supernatural is seen as a sign of their ignorance or barbarism. Or so the modern perceives. But then the modern perceives very little because he is covered with too many artificial accretions to be able to experience, and therefore perceive, the real.

The modern is right in one respect at least. He is right in perceiving that the Anglo-Saxons were primitives. He is right, however, for the wrong reasons. His error lies in his perception that the primitive is synonymous with the barbaric or the ignorant. In point of fact, the Anglo-Saxons are primitive while he, the modern, is barbaric and ignorant. One who is primitive is one who never loses sight of the prime realities, the first things, upon which all else rests. As an adjective *prime* relates to the chief things, the most important things; as a noun it means the state of highest perfection. A primitive never loses sight of the most important things nor of the state of highest perfection which, properly understood, is the Godhead. It is the ignorant and the barbarian who lose sight of these things.

Let us leave the modern to his barbarism and ignorance, and let us return to the healthy wyrdness of the Anglo-Saxons. The conclusion of "The Seafarer" is the conclusion that any sagacious Primitive will draw as the primal lesson of life. It is a lesson that needs to be learned from life before death forces its conclusion upon us.

> A man may bury his brother with the dead
> and strew his grave with the golden things
> he would have him take, treasures of all kinds,
> but gold hoarded when he here lived
> cannot allay the anger of God
> towards a soul sin-freighted.

5

Dante: Assent's Ascent

Lovers of the Great Books argue interminably about which is the greatest. Among philosophers, the argument might focus on the relative merits of the works of Plato and Aristotle, or of Augustine and Aquinas. Among lovers of literature, some will argue that Homer's epics are the greatest; others, possibly, though perhaps less convincingly, that Virgil deserves the laurel. And then there are those who will insist that Shakespeare is as good as it gets. And yet, for Catholics, we can hardly leave Dante out of the discussion. From a purely Catholic literary perspective he must surely stand supreme. He is to Catholic literature what Thomas Aquinas is to Catholic philosophy. If Thomas is rightly called the Angelic Doctor, might Dante deserve to be called the Angelic Poet?

If this is so, we can say that Dante's *Divine Comedy* must be seen as an indispensable part of every good Catholic's reading list. The problem is that Dante's *magnum opus* must be read with Catholic eyes and not with the eyes with which the modern reader so often reads it. The problem with the modern reading of the poem is that it tends to remain trapped in Hell, never venturing forth into Purgatory and Paradise. This is a consequence of the way that Dante has been read and taught for decades—indeed, for centuries.

Ever since the Reformation, it has been the tendency to teach and read the *Inferno* to the exclusion of the *Purgatorio* and the *Paradiso*. The reason is obvious enough. Protestants believed in Hell but not in Purgatory. As for Paradise, the Protestant idea of Heaven precluded the hierarchy of the communion of saints which Dante presents in his *Comedy*. Since Dante's Purgatory and Paradise were considered to be heretical, the Protestants were left with nothing but his Hell in which to wallow. Disagreeing with Dante about the nature of the Divine Light, the Protestants could at least agree with him with regard to the darkness which is the consequence of its absence.

The tendency to read the *Inferno* to the exclusion of the *Purgatorio* and the *Paradiso* was continued by the children of the self-named Enlightenment. Whereas these sceptic-souled secularists might not believe in Hell any more than they believed in Purgatory or Heaven, they could at least see that evil existed—even if they no longer called it sin, and they could perceive its harmful consequences. As such the *Inferno* still resonated psychologically, even if its theology was now ignored.

It might be argued that none of the foregoing is of much concern to Catholics. If the Protestants and secularists want to wallow in Dante's Hell because they have excluded themselves from Purgatory and Heaven, that is their problem. Of what concern is it to us? The problem is that even the Catholic schools are also often stuck in Hell, having excluded themselves from Purgatory and Heaven. It is sad but true that only Dante's *Inferno* is on the curriculum at many otherwise good Catholic schools.

Why is this?

In part it is because we have bought the Protestant and secularist misperception that the *Inferno* is far superior to the other two books of the *Commedia*. This is quite simply not the case. It was not the view of the poet who composed it, nor of those who understand the poem best. Take, for instance, the judgment of Maurice Baring, one of the most cultured and well-read men of the last century:

> Scaling the circles of the *Paradiso*, we are conscious the whole time of an ascent not only in the quality of the substance but in that of the form. It is a long perpetual crescendo, increasing in beauty until the final consummation in the very last line. Somebody once defined an artist . . . as a man who knows how to finish things. If this definition is true—and I think it is—then Dante was the greatest artist who ever lived. His final canto is the best, and it depends on and completes the beginning.[1]

Having seen through the lie, or at least the misconception born of ignorance, that the *Inferno* is superior to the other two books of the *Commedia*, why, one wonders, do some Catholic schools still not teach the *Purgatorio* and the *Paradiso*? An all too common reason is that the teachers are only teaching what they were taught. Since those who teach were only taught the *Inferno*, they only know the *Inferno*. It is, therefore, easier to stay in one's own comfort zone (in this case, ironically, Hell!) rather than venture forth into unknown and uncharted territory. Literarily, if not literally, the path of least resistance for many Catholic teachers leads to Hell—and, what is worse, having led there it stays there.

A final reason for sometimes only teaching the *Inferno* is that there is simply not enough time to teach the whole *Commedia*. Sadly, this is usually true. And yet, if this is so, why not teach the *Purgatorio* or the *Paradiso*, and not the *Inferno*? Better still, why not select certain cantos from each of the three books, thereby at least giving the students a sense of the majesty and integrity of the whole work?

Regardless of the degree to which the world is only at home in Hell, it is imperative that Catholics assent to the

---

1   Maurice Baring, *Have You Anything to Declare?* (London: William Heinemann Ltd, 1936), 106.

ascent which leads from Hell, via Mount Purgatory, into the celestial spheres of Paradise. Where else should Catholics seek to be than in the presence of God and his saints? Why accept anything less, still less the ultimate "less" which is God's infernal absence?

Although *The Divine Comedy* is possibly the greatest poem ever written, it is not without its problems, or dare one say flaws, especially in the way that the poet consigns real-life people to Hell. Is he not committing the sin of detraction against these people? Is he not causing scandal by putting popes and other known people in Hell? What are we supposed to do with this? Just ignore it? Call it poetic license?

These are great questions that deserve and indeed demand answers.

Our discomfort with what might be termed Dante's judgmentalism is understandable. None of us should presume that anyone is in Hell. It is fair, therefore, to question this aspect of Dante's approach. In his defence, we might suggest that he wanted to avoid writing a crudely formal allegory about the deadly sins which would have been the case had he presented them as personified abstractions. In putting real people in Hell and Purgatory, it enlivens his story, bringing it to life literarily. He is, therefore, employing poetic licence. Whether this is sufficient reason for the crime of judgmentalism is, however, questionable. Might he not have been better served had he peopled his afterlife with fictional characters of his own invention, suggestive perhaps and inspired no doubt by real life historical people, but not actually naming them and therefore damning them (at least literarily)? If he had done this, he would not only have avoided the sin of judgmentalism but would have saved generations of readers from having to read the historical context surrounding the real-life people whom he consigns to Hell or Purgatory.

Needless to say, there would be no problem with his naming of the canonized saints in Paradise, but the irony is that Dante actually places a canonized saint in Hell! He consigns Saint Celestine V to the vestibule of Hell for what he termed Celestine's "great refusal" to accept and embrace the papal office. Although Dante does not name Celestine V directly as the "coward" who made the "great refusal," it has been accepted by most critics that Celestine was indeed the "cowardly" soul whom he singles out for his scorn. It seems that Dante vents his spleen against Celestine, not so much for his resignation *per se* but for the fact that his resignation had enabled Dante's enemy, Boniface VIII, to become pope.

Leaving aside the problem with his naming of specific real-life popes and priests, Dante would be doing nothing wrong in placing fictional popes and priests in Hell and Purgatory. There have been many bad popes and priests, and it is good to embrace and acknowledge the fact. Good Christians should not be afraid to admit that there are bad Christians, including bad priests and popes. Indeed, the paradox is that good Christians know that they are themselves bad Christians.

It is, however, imperative that we not allow this tragic flaw in Dante's comedy to blind us to the beauty of the great poet's engagement with sin (in Hell and Purgatory), with repentance (in Purgatory), and with sanctity (in Heaven). It is a majestic work, filled to the brim with Christian insight into man's relationship with God and neighbour. In short, we should not allow the mote in Dante's eye to become the plank in ours.

Before we leave our discussion of Dante's *Divine Comedy*, we should also address the thorny question of which edition should be read.

The present author strongly recommends either of two editions. The first is the Dorothy L. Sayers translation (Penguin Classics), and the other is the more recent translation by Anthony Esolen (Modern Library Classics). A singular strength of the Sayers translation is its adherence to Dante's original *terza rima*, the rhyme scheme that Dante invented for the poem.

This verse stanza form, consisting of interlocking three-line stanzas connected in a single canto-length chain, is formally robust and conveys a cohesive strength to the fabric of the work. Something integral to the poem is lost when the *terza rima* is abandoned by translators. The problem is that it is much easier to find words that rhyme in Italian than it is in English, making *terza rima* difficult to render from the one language into the other. In her determination to adhere to Dante's formal rhyme scheme, Sayers is sometimes forced to compromise the quality of the verse. It is for this reason, presumably, that Anthony Esolen, following the lead of most other translators of the *Commedia*, chooses to forsake *terza rima* in order to be more faithful to the qualitative rendering of the verse. Should his translation be selected, it would be helpful were the reader to seek out at least a sample passage of the Sayers translation to gain some sense of the formal structure of the poem.

Another strength of these two particular editions is the quality of the explanatory notes. It is simply not possible for a modern reader to fully appreciate Dante's work without frequent reference to the accompanying notes. The quality of such notes is, therefore, crucial. Especially important is the manner in which the notes conform with Dante's Thomistic understanding of the cosmos and man's place within it. Sayers is especially good at making that connection.

Any diligent reader seeking to do some further background reading as a means of delving deeper into the *Commedia* could do far worse than to consult *The Passionate Intellect: Dorothy L. Sayers' Encounter with Dante* by Barbara Reynolds (Kent State University Press, 1989). Dr. Reynolds was a close friend of Sayers. It was she who finished Sayers's translation of the *Paradiso* after Sayers had died in the midst of the work. She is, therefore, uniquely placed to guide us into a deeper encounter with this greatest of poets.

And one parting thought. It is an intriguing fact that the Italian language has moved in slow motion in its development over the centuries, at least as compared to English. For this reason, Dante's Italian is much closer to modern Italian than, for instance, is Chaucer's English to modern English. In fact, Dante is as easy to read in the original, if one knows Italian, as is Shakespeare's English to a modern English reader, even though Shakespeare is writing three hundred years after Dante and therefore three hundred years closer to us in time. This intriguing fact is mentioned because those who speak Italian might want to try reading the poem in the original tongue in which it was written, which is always best. Might it even be suggested that it is worth learning Italian simply to be able to enjoy this most wonderful of poets in the language in which he writes?

6

Chaucer: The Pilgrim Muse

He is the poet of the dawn, who wrote
  The Canterbury Tales, and his old age
  Made beautiful with song; and as I read
I hear the crowing cock, I hear the note
  Of lark and linnet, and from every page
  Rise odours of plough'd field or flowery mead.
                              Henry Wadsworth Longfellow

Chaucer was a poet who came at the end of the medieval
age and order . . . the final fruit and inheritor of that
order . . . he was much more sane and cheerful and normal
than most of the later writers. He was less delirious than
Shakespeare, less harsh than Milton, less fanatical than
Bunyan, less embittered than Swift.
                              G. K. Chesterton[1]

Much has changed in the six hundred years that separate
late mediaeval England and the "postmodern" world.
Theologically, we have passed from Christian orthodoxy,
via heresy, to godless hedonism. Philosophically, we have
passed from realism, via nominalism, to radical relativism.

---

1   G. K. Chesterton, *Chaucer* (New York: Farrar and Rinehart, 1932), 12.

Politically, we have passed from monarchy, via regicide and republicanism, to a plutocracy which masquerades as a democracy. Economically, we have passed from feudal agrarianism, via Machiavellian manipulation and mercantile industrialism, to global consumerism. Technologically, we have passed from plough and scythe, via steam and electricity, to outer space and cyberspace.

But a closer look is warranted.

Theologically, Christian orthodoxy is unchanged and is as true today as it was in Chaucer's time. Philosophically, realism still reflects reality regardless of the relative rise of relativism. Politically, power is still centralized in the hands of Big Government, which uses it in its own interest and to the detriment of the interests of the relatively powerless majority. Economically, the real health and wealth of the people is still rooted ultimately in the fruits of the earth and the way in which that fruit is harvested by the tilling of the land and the toiling of labour. Technologically, nothing has changed except the tools with which we toil and the toys with which we play. We are not defined or changed in any major or meaningful way by our tools and our toys, nor is real reality changed by virtual reality.

Plus ça change, plus c'est la même chose. Nothing essential has changed, which means that everything essentially remains the same.

In Chaucer's *Canterbury Tales*, we see essentially the same unchanging humanity struggling with essentially the same unchanging problems. We see the same struggle between holiness and hedonism, sanctity and sin, virtue and vice. The seven deadly sins are as deadly now as they were in Chaucer's time. They kill human society as surely as they kill the human soul. They destroy the love of God and neighbour as surely as they destroy the wholeness or holiness of the self-centred self. Pride is still pride, and it still precedes a fall; lust is still lust, and it is as destructive to life and to marriage as it always was; avarice is still avarice, gluttony is still gluttony, sloth is still sloth, envy is still envy, wrath is still wrath, *ad nauseam, ad infinitum*. In Chaucer, as in Dante, we see Everyman, which is to say all of us, struggling with the perennial problems that have beset every generation of men throughout the countless centuries of human history.

Nothing has changed, everything remains the same. *Plus ça change . . .*

Not only does Chaucer know this axiomatic and essential truth, it is the very animating principle of his Muse. *The Canterbury Tales* is an engagement with the essential truth of the Gospel, in opposition to the Hell of hedonism and the concupiscent cornucopia of deadly delights that it offers, and also an engagement with the essential truth of realism, in opposition to the proto-relativism of nominalism.[2]

As with *The Aeneid* of Virgil, *The Canterbury Tales* is an unfinished work, its author dying before it could be brought to full fruition. On the one hand, we have only fragments of a much bigger work; on the other hand, the fragments are themselves finished tales, told by the various pilgrims as they journey together on pilgrimage to Canterbury. All of the tales are worth reading, and all of them convey edifying Christian morality, but we will concentrate on the General Prologue to the whole work and on just one of the tales, "The Nun's Priest's Tale."

The General Prologue begins with an evocation of resurrected life. It is April and sweet showers help to bring new life to every wood and field. This sets the scene for the resurrected spirit of people longing to go on pilgrimage. One such group of pilgrims meets by chance at an inn in London and decide to journey together to Canterbury, telling each other

---

2   A good study of Chaucer's philosophical realism and its engagement with nominalism is David Williams's *Language Redeemed: Chaucer's Mature Poetry* (Naples, FL: Sapientia Press, 2007).

stories along the way. We are then introduced to the pilgrims, who are a motley group comprised mostly of reprobates who are evidently in need of the grace that a pilgrimage brings. There is the Knight, a man of courage and martial prowess, who joins the pilgrimage as an act of thanksgiving, having returned from the wars; there is the Knight's son, the Squire, who has the courage of his father in battle but is altogether a dandy in times of peace, wearing the most fashionable clothes and hairstyle and delighting in music and dance. There is the less than holy Prioress who is too prim and proper for her own good, seeking the pleasures that opulence affords. Even worse than the prim Prioress is the worldly Monk, whose wealth makes a mockery of his vow of poverty and whose heretical theology makes a mockery of his orthodox pretensions. As if the Prioress and Monk were not cause enough for scandal, the Friar plumbs new depths of depravity, committing acts of fornication and adultery, getting maidens pregnant, and begging from the rich so that he can keep up his life of lechery and luxury. The roll call of reprobates continues: the shady Merchant, the pleasure-seeking Franklin, the avaricious Physician, the formidable and self-serving Wife of Bath, the utterly uncouth Miller, the dishonest Manciple, the corrupt and lecherous Summoner, and last and perhaps worst, the corrupt Pardoner who makes a living selling fake relics to the gullible faithful. And yet in the midst of this doom and despondency, Chaucer kindles candles of sanctity to lighten our hearts and enlighten our way. There is the conscientious Clerk, or student, who prefers poverty and a life of learning over the comforts of the world. There is, especially and magnificently, the poor Parson, who exemplifies the calling of a good and holy priest, putting his hypocritical neighbours to shame with his life of simple service to the farthest flung members of his flock; and there is his brother, the Ploughman, who, living in peace and perfect charity, loving God above all, is the epitome of a truly holy layman. And so it is that Chaucer seasons his largely objectionable menagerie of miserable sinners with a couple of saints, one representing the clergy and the other the laity, who serve as candles in the dark, shining forth sanity and sanctity in the midst of the mayhem of the madness of sin.

If the General Prologue should be essential reading for every Catholic, or at least those lines which depict the holiness of the Parson and the Ploughman, most people will not have the leisure or the liberty to read all of the Tales that the pilgrims tell on their way to Canterbury. We will look at just one of the many that we might have selected, "The Nun's Priest's Tale," in the hope that it will serve to whet the reader's appetite for more.

"The Nun's Priest's Tale" is a fable about a rooster called Chauntecleer and his favourite hen, whose name is Pertelote. As with the more famous fables of Aesop, this fable has a definite moral message. Chauntecleer has a nightmare in which he has the vision of a villainous fox, its tail and both ears tipped with black to give it diabolically symbolic features. There then follows a discourse by Pertelote on dreams in which she dismisses them on essentially materialistic grounds as being meaningless, to which Chauntecleer responds with a lengthy riposte in which he cites biblical sources for the prophetic power to be gleaned from dream visions. The Tale contains ironic references to the Fall of Adam, not least because the whole fable is essentially a retelling of the story of man's fall. Chauntecleer can be seen to represent Adam and his seven wives would appear to signify the seven deadly sins, with Pertelote, as the first and favourite of the seven, representing Pride. In the midst of the rambunctious humour with which the tale is replete, there is a deeply theological meditation on the relationship between predestination and the freedom of the will. As the story unfolds, Chauntecleer, in the symbolic role of Adam, is tempted by a real-life diabolical fox, who flatters the rooster, playing on his pride. Having trapped Chauntecleer in his jaws, the fox falls through the foolishness of his own pride, enabling Chauntecleer to escape and fly up into a tree, symbolic of the Cross of Christ. We see, therefore, in this one tale the whimsical and wistful melding of *levitas* and *gravitas* that caused Chesterton to praise so effusively Chaucer's cheerfulness and sanity.

Before we leave our discussion of *The Canterbury Tales*, we should consider Chaucer's English, which is called Middle English, to distinguish it from the Old English in which the *Beowulf* poet writes and the modern English that comes after it. Whereas the Old English of *Beowulf* is very Germanic and very foreign to modern English speakers, the English of Chaucer is recognizable, at least with a modicum of effort. It is, however, more difficult to read than Shakespeare, who writes in Early Modern English, so many readers might find it very challenging. For this reason, an interlinear translation, which contains a modern translation side by side with the original text, will enable the reader to compare the Middle English original with the modern version.

Readers should also be warned that some of Chaucer's Tales are bawdy, "The Miller's Tale" especially. Even though the overarching moral of these tales is profoundly Christian, some readers may be offended by the way in which some of them are told.

As we leave our discussion of mediaeval literature, we should ponder again and anew the essentially unchanging nature of man and his relationship with God and neighbour, adding a cautionary word about those "regressives" who believe that there was a "golden age" in the past. Certain types of "neo-mediaevalists" fall into this category. For such "regressives" everything was wonderful in the middle ages. They point with due reverence to Chartres Cathedral and show due deference to the monastic and mendicant orders that proliferated in mediaeval times. This is all to the good. Only a philistine fails to appreciate the majesty of the Gothic, and only a scoundrel pours scorn upon the religious life. Yet one perusal of Dante's divinely inspired *Comedy* or Chaucer's perambulatory *Tales* will dissuade anyone from seeing the middle ages as a "golden age." For every mediaeval saint in Dante's Paradise, there is a corresponding mediaeval sinner in his Hell. For every San Paolo and San Francesco there is a Paolo and Francesca. For every saintly mediaeval Parson on Chaucer's Pilgrimage there is a dastardly Pardoner; for every honest Ploughman there is a dishonest Miller. The litany of sin and scandal is as horrific in the middle ages as in any other age.

For this reason, the middle ages should not be studied as an outdated artefact, or as a mere *curio*. On the contrary, the middle ages are very much alive in the sense that they accurately reflect undying truths. Where the middle ages are right they are extremely right, as in the faith of St. Francis or the philosophy of Aquinas. This union of *fides et ratio* resonates through all ages with the romance of realism. On the other hand, where the middle ages are wrong, they are extremely wrong, as in the corruption and tyranny of many mediaeval rulers. Yet even the errors of the middle ages teach us valuable lessons about the corruption and tyranny endemic to rulers in all ages.

To see as Chaucer sees is not merely to see reality as a late mediaeval Englishman saw it, but to see reality as it is.

7

Thomas More and Utopian Literature

Moving forward from the late fourteenth century to the early sixteenth, and from what historians call the late mediaeval to the early modern period of history, we come to the towering figure and presence of St. Thomas More. Much could and should be said of this saint and martyr, but we are going to focus solely on the importance of his fictional work, *Utopia*, published in 1516, which can be considered the progenitor of the genre of utopian fiction, as well as being a major milestone in the evolution of fantasy literature in general.

The fact that "utopia," as employed by More, means "no place" or "nowhere" (from the Greek *ou*, meaning "not," and *topos*, meaning "place") as opposed to "good place" (from the Greek *eu*, meaning "good," and *topos*, meaning "place") is a fact all too often forgotten by modern critics who lack the subtlety to see the true intent of More's satire. Supposing that More meant *eutopia* not *outopia*, these critics have concluded quite erroneously that More was more of a humanist than he was a Christian or, even more absurdly, that he was a proto-communist. For a man who willingly laid down his life for his friends and his faith, such conclusions lack all credibility. Although More used the medium of Christian fantasy as a vehicle for voicing criticisms of the cruelty and corruption of the times in which he lived, his purpose in writing the satire went beyond the temporal to the eternal. In the final analysis, More's *outopia* can be seen much more as a *dystopia* than a *eutopia*, depicting a world of self-evident absurdities based upon erroneous conceptions of reality, though woven within this dystopian framework are what might be called eu-topian elements, such as the importance placed on the contemplative life and the efforts made to counter the evils of avarice.

In writing his *Utopia* More established a whole new genre of fantasy literature, the utopian or dystopian fantasy, in which imaginary worlds are created as a reflection or as a way of seeing the real world. From Swift's *Gulliver's Travels* to Orwell's *Nineteen Eighty-Four*, More's originality has inspired generations of writers to hold a utopian mirror to the world in which they lived.

Gulliver's Travels by the eighteenth-century author Jonathan Swift developed the utopian genre into what is perhaps the progenitor of science fiction. Swift introduces us to weird alien creatures, such as the platonic equine houyhnhnms and the bestial humanoid yahoos, and presents us with the "scientific" wonders of floating islands and the "scientific" blunders of mad scientists. Yet he was not writing merely to exercise a scientific imagination but to exorcise the nonsense of modernism and scientism, the latter of which might be defined as the idolizing of the physical sciences as the arbiter of all truth. Swift, a profoundly tradition-oriented Christian, used science in his fiction to expose the follies of the emergent scientism of his day. In doing so, he established a tradition, which many subsequent authors followed, in which science fiction, for all its use of science in the modern sense, is informed by science in the older, traditional sense. It is theology and philosophy that inform and inspire the best science fiction, regardless of how many spaceships, time machines, and five-legged aliens are employed in the plot.

As for the ongoing tradition of utopian literature, later utopian writers follow in More's footsteps in terms of etymology, using the term as being literally "no-place." This is seen in the titles of Victorian utopian literature, such as William Morris's *News from Nowhere* and Samuel Butler's *Erewhon*, an anagram of "nowhere." Far from being a "good place," most of the great utopian visions in literature have been dystopian, which means "bad-place," from the Greek *dus* (bad) and *topos* (place). We think perhaps, in twentieth-century literature, of three great works of dystopian literature: *Lord of the World* by Robert Hugh Benson, *Brave New World* by Aldous Huxley, and *Nineteen Eighty-Four* by George Orwell. Although only the first of this triumvirate of novels was written by a Catholic, all three of them serve as timely warnings of how secularist ideas lead to nightmare realities.

But are such utopian visions important enough to warrant our concern? Should we care whether an imaginary place is good or bad? Is it not literally "nowhere," in the sense that it does not exist? Why concern ourselves with such fantasies about worlds which are the fertile or furtive figments of a writer's dreams or nightmares? Should we not keep our feet firmly grounded in the real world in which we live and not allow our heads to drift into the clouds of neverland?

It is in the consideration of these questions that the distinction between the various etymological definitions of utopia becomes important. Neverland might be nowhere (ou-topia), but is there an ultimate good place (eu-topia), a foreverland where good people live happily ever after? In other words, is there a truth to be found in fiction, or in fairy tales, or in utopian fantasies?

In one sense, such questions can be answered in utilitarian terms. The fact is that we need to be shown visions of the person we are meant to be and also visions of the society in which we are meant to live. As Christ, the Perfect Person, shows us who we *should* be; utopia, insofar as it is genuinely *eu*-topia, shows us the sort of society in which we *should* live.

Although we will never be perfect as Christ is perfect, we are nonetheless called to strive towards perfection, which is the call to holiness. Similarly, although we will never have Heaven on earth, we should strive to bring earth closer to Heaven, which is the call to make the earth a better place, a good place—*eu*topia. The fact that we are miserable sinners does not mean that we should not take the Sinless One as our model; the fact that our society is full of miserable sinners, ourselves included, does not mean that we should not strive to make our society a *good place*. Even if the frailty and sinfulness of fallen human nature will mean that the good place to which we strive will never be a perfect place, it is sufficient to know that efforts towards the *good* place generally make the world a *better* place.

It is for this reason that the eu-topian visions of great writers, such as J. R. R. Tolkien, who shows us an agrarian utopia in his depiction of the Shire, should be valued as a source of inspiration that leads to the aspiration to make our own world a better place. There are, however, other ways of showing us utopia, such as the way of satire adopted by More in his *Utopia* and by Swift in *Gulliver's Travels*. These great satirists show us *ou*-topia, "nowhere," as a scathingly satirical mirror of our own world caricatured through the process of *reductio ad absurdum*. In seeing our own corrupt society in ugly and absurd caricature, we are shocked out of our complacent comfort zones into seeking a better and more just society. In this sense the satirical depiction of *ou*-topia inspires the vision of *eu*-topia.

The other means of inspiring the desire for eu-topia are via the *via negativa* of dystopian fiction, such as in the aforementioned works by Benson, Huxley, and Orwell. These authors present us with visions of the bad-place that could become reality if certain inherent tendencies in our own world are not countered and checked. In Benson's dystopia we see the dangers of secularism and the rise of the popular demagogue;

in Huxley we see the dangers of hedonism and the heedless numbness of comfort-addiction; in Orwell we see the inherent corruption in socialist revolution and the ominous potential that the modern world presents for globalist tyranny. In being shown these cautionary scenarios of the way things *could* be (dystopia), we are inspired to a better understanding of the way they *should* be (eutopia).

It goes without saying that our understanding of what is good determines our understanding of what is a good society. If we have a false and fallacious understanding of the good, our utopian dreams will metamorphose into dystopian nightmares. This is what happened to the utopian dreams of Rousseau, whose "noble savage" transformed vampire-like into the ignoble savagery of the French Revolution and the Reign of Terror that followed in its wake. This is what happened to the utopian dreams of Marx whose dictatorship of the proletariat collapsed into the dictatorship of the politicians and the mass murder that they instigated. This is what is happening as the utopian dreams of radical relativism turn into the eugenic nightmare of institutionalized infanticide (abortion) and institutionalized geriatricide (euthanasia).

In the midst of the madness of so many dystopias, real and imagined, it is the vision of eutopia which shows us the vision of sanity which keeps us sane.

The only alternative to eutopia or dystopia is myopia, the short-sighted pragmatism that refuses to see beyond the present-day. This pragmatic near-sightedness, masquerading as realism, puts its trust in the myopia of the market, which has no way of measuring or seeing anything but the present, and the myopia of our media-manipulated "democracy," which has no inclination to see beyond the next election. It places its trust in an untried and untested globalist future, the consequences of which it cannot fathom, but refuses to see the past and the long-sighted and tried and tested lessons it teaches. Ultimately this myopia is no real alternative to eutopia because it leads inexorably to dystopia. It is the path of least resistance which leads to Hell, and not merely the Hell in the hereafter but the Hell in the here and now. Only the blind and the foolish take such a path. The rest of us are keeping our eyes on the good place!

8

Shakespeare

He was not of an age, but for all time!
Ben Jonson on William Shakespeare

These famous words of praise by the great poet, Ben Jonson, in honour of the even greater poet, William Shakespeare, were published in the First Folio edition of Shakespeare's plays in 1623, only seven years after his death. The words of praise have, therefore, become words of prophecy because none of the Bard of Avon's contemporaries could have foreseen the extent to which Shakespeare would conquer the world in the centuries after his death. Today, he stands as a colossus who straddles the centuries, towering above all other writers, with the possible exception of Homer and Dante. His stature as a giant of civilisation is itself sufficient reason to read, watch, and study his works. In spending time with Shakespeare, we are communing with genius. Can there be many better and more fruitful and edifying ways of spending our time?

There is, however, another and deeper meaning behind Ben Jonson's words. It is not merely that Shakespeare has survived the test of time, it is that his plays, and the truth and morality contained within them, transcend time. They are not merely works that endure *in* time, they are works that are *beyond* time. They have their inspiration in eternal verities and they point to those same verities. Such truths do not change with time, nor are they changed by it. They simply *are*.

Perhaps the best way of illustrating this extra-temporal dimension to Shakespeare is to compare the *Heilige Geist* with the *zeitgeist*, the Holy Spirit with the Spirit of the Age. The Holy Spirit does not change from one generation to the next. He simply *is*. The Spirit of the Age, on the other hand, is always changing. It is subject to time and is changed by it. The literal meaning of *zeitgeist* is Time-Spirit. One who serves the Time-Spirit is one who wants to seem relevant to the fads and fashions of his own day. He is primarily concerned with being up-to-date. The problem is that those who are up-to-date are very soon out of date because, as C. S. Lewis quipped, fashions are always coming and going, but mostly going. One who is relevant to the fashions of today will be irrelevant to the fashions of tomorrow.

The reason that Shakespeare is not of an age but for all time is that he serves the *Heilige Geist* and not the *zeitgeist*. The truths that inspire his muse, and the truths that emerge in the fruits of his muse (his plays and poems), are the truths of the Holy Spirit, the truths of the Trinity, the truths of Christ, and the truths of the Catholic Church, which is Christ's Mystical Body.[1] Such truths do not merely stand the test of time. They are the very truths by which time itself is tested.

These metaphysical first principles are crucial to our understanding of why we should read and learn Shakespeare, or indeed why we should read and learn anything else that contains goodness, truth, and beauty. Such things point us towards eternity and helps us to get there.

Lest we be tempted to think that the foregoing discussion means that the reading of Shakespeare is purely a spiritual or

---

1   There is much evidence to show that Shakespeare was a believing Catholic in very anti-Catholic times. See, for instance, the present author's *The Quest for Shakespeare: The Bard of Avon and the Church of Rome* (San Francisco: Ignatius Press, 2008).

mystical undertaking, connected solely to what theologians call the anagogical meaning of life, we should remind ourselves of the paradox that the timeless is always timely. If the timeless resides in the eternal, then all times are present to it. If it is timeless, it is always true—and if it is always true, then it is always relevant. It is for this reason that Shakespeare's works are rightly listed amongst the "permanent things," those things which *are* and will always *be*, and, in consequence, those things that are and will always be relevant.

Let us look at a few of the truths in Shakespeare that are also and always timely.

In *Romeo and Juliet* the difference between true and false love, that is, rational and irrational love, is highlighted. The sobering lesson that the play teaches is that the thing possessed possesses the possessor. This is evident in Romeo's blasphemous remark in which he exclaims that "heaven is here / Where Juliet lives." Juliet is Romeo's alpha and omega, his beginning and his end. She is the goddess to which he owes the sum of all his worship. It is for this reason that he chooses this "heaven" even when it becomes his Hell. In Dante's *Inferno*, the lustful are described as "those who make reason slave to appetite" or as those who let their erotic passions "master reason and good sense." Like Paolo and Francesca in the *Inferno*, Shakespeare's lovers have overthrown reason in pursuit of passion. Embracing their madness and blindness, their "love" has surrendered to the force of feeling. Their love is headless and therefore heedless of the bad consequences of the bad choices being made. Shakespeare and Dante, both believing Catholics, are well aware of the danger of separating love from reason. Love must be subject to reason; a love that denies or defies reason is illicit and is not really love at all.

In some ways, *Romeo and Juliet* can be seen as a cautionary commentary on the two great commandments of Christ that we love the Lord our God and that we love our neighbour.

The two lovers deny the love of God in their deification of each other, with disastrous consequences, and their respective families deny the love of neighbour in their vengeful feuding. It could be said that the venereal and vengeful passions of Verona represent the culture of death in microcosm. A society that turns its back on Christ and his commandments is on the path to suicide, to its self-annihilation. If the lessons are not learned and the warnings heeded, the sinful society will be doomed to be damned.

Similar lessons to those taught in *Romeo and Juliet* are taught in *The Merchant of Venice*, in which the test of the caskets shows that true love is about dying to oneself so that one can give oneself fully and self-sacrificially to the beloved. This true love is contrasted with the self-centred desire of those who fail the test. In a similar vein, the test of the rings at the end of the play reinforces the necessity of self-sacrifice in the Sacrament of Marriage. Finally, of course, Portia's wisdom reminds us that we must love our neighbour, showing the quality of mercy that God has shown to us.

In *Julius Caesar*, Shakespeare pours scorn on Caesar's vanity, on Antony's bloodthirsty opportunism, on Cassius's ambition, and on Brutus's misguided idealism. Yet he is not cursing from the perspective of a worldly cynicism but from that of a believing Christian at a time when believing Christians were being tortured and put to death by the vanity of monarchs, by bloodthirsty opportunists, by political ambition, and by misguided idealism.

There is, however, a deeper level of meaning in *Julius Caesar* that is all too often overlooked completely. It is the sound of silence within the play, the scream in the vacuum of the play's vacuity. It is the unheard and unheeded voice of the virtuous. It is the voice of Calpurnia, which, if heeded, would have saved Caesar's life; it is the voice of Portia, which, if heeded, might have urged Brutus to think twice about his involvement with the conspirators. It is the voice of the Soothsayer and of the augurers. It is the voice of Artemidorus, a teacher of rhetoric, whose note to Caesar is devoid of all rhetorical devices and direct to the point of bluntness. The note is not read, the voices are not heard, and the consequences are fatal. All that was missing in the play is the one thing necessary: the still, small voice of virtue and wisdom that the proud refuse to hear.

The whole of *Hamlet* turns on the crucial distinction between reason and will, and between that which is and that which seems to be, and the test of success is the extent to which the protagonists conform their will to reason. This is Hamlet's struggle throughout the play. In the end, through conforming his will to reason and in connecting reason to faith, he becomes the willing minister of Divine Providence, bringing justice to the wicked King Claudius and restoring justice to the realm. The fact that Hamlet has to lay down his own life in order to restore such justice turns him into a Christ figure, an association that Shakespeare makes apparent through Hamlet's allusion to Scripture and through the employment of poison as a metaphor for sin.

In many ways, Macbeth can be seen as an anti-Hamlet. Hamlet begins in the Slough of Despond, temperamentally tempted to despair, but grows in virtue throughout the play until he reaches the ripeness of Christian conversion and the readiness to accept his own death as part of God's benign Providence. Macbeth, on the other hand, begins as a lionized hero, but falls into the folly of sin, prompted by a demonic promise of worldly power, and ends as a deranged nihilist denying the meaning of anything. Hamlet grows in faith because he grows in reason; Macbeth loses his faith because he loses his reason.

In a more general sense, the dynamism of the underlying dialectic in Shakespeare's plays, and therefore of the dialogue, is centred on the tension between Christian conscience and self-serving, cynical secularism. Whereas the heroes and heroines of

Shakespearean drama are informed by an orthodox Christian understanding of virtue, the villains are normally moral relativists and Machiavellian practitioners of secular *real-politik*.

In the final analysis, the right reason for reading Shakespeare is to learn the right reason that Shakespeare teaches.

9

Cervantes

Cervantes on his galley sets the sword back in the sheath
(Don John of Austria rides homeward with a wreath.)
And he sees across a weary land a straggling road in Spain,
Up which a lean and foolish knight forever rides in vain,
And he smiles, but not as Sultans smile,
*   and settles back the blade . . .*

G. K. Chesterton (Lepanto)

In his marvellous poem *Lepanto*, G. K. Chesterton imagined the great Spanish writer, Miguel de Cervantes, setting his sword back in his sheath and smiling contentedly after he has played his part in the historic victory of the Christian fleet over its Turkish foe at the Battle of Lepanto. Chesterton concluded his poem with these lines as a way of showing that the victory was crucial to the survival of Christendom and its cultural fruits, epitomized and symbolized by Cervantes's classic novel, *Don Quixote*, about a lean and foolish knight who forever rides in vain. Chesterton's point was that Christendom might have been destroyed and overrun by the forces of Islam had not the Christian fleet prevailed, in which case works such as those of Cervantes (and indeed of Chesterton himself) would never have been written or published.

Miguel de Cervantes fought heroically at Lepanto, receiving a serious wound to his left hand which he would wear as a badge of honour for the remainder of his life, as well he might. Born in Spain in 1547, Cervantes's early life reads like a swashbuckling adventure story. Having fought at Lepanto in 1571, he was captured by Barbary pirates four years later and imprisoned for five years, making several daring escape attempts before finally being rescued by the Trinitarian friars in 1580. Thereafter his life became uneventful, marked only by his frustrated attempts to make a name for himself as a writer and playwright. By the time that he finally attained success with the publication of the first part of *Don Quixote* in 1605, he was fifty-eight years old. The second part would appear ten years later, a year before his death. Cervantes was, therefore, a late bloomer and what might be called a one-hit wonder, his other works being largely unsuccessful during his own lifetime and largely forgotten today.

If, however, Cervantes can only claim one literary classic to his name, as distinct from the dozens of classics written by his great contemporary Shakespeare, he can claim to have written the most successful work of literature in the history of the world, at least in terms of global sales. It is generally accepted that Don Quixote is the all-time bestseller, outselling its nearest rivals, *A Tale of Two Cities* by Dickens and *The Lord of the Rings* by Tolkien. As for its literary merit, we can trust the view of Maurice Baring, a fine writer who was himself the finest of critics, that "no book has such a good beginning as *Don Quixote*, and no book has a finer end."[1]

So what makes *Don Quixote* so special?

First, if not necessarily foremost, it was a first of its kind, arguably the first novel ever written, the progenitor of a whole new literary form. It is full of exciting action and is driven by

---

1   Baring, *Have You Anything to Declare?*, 195.

the unlikely friendship of Don Quixote and his servant and travelling companion, Sancho Panza, the latter's almost cynical no-nonsense realism serving as an intellectual foil to Quixote's manically romantic fantasizing. At the novel's heart is the evident desire of Cervantes to satirize and lampoon the popular books of chivalry, the *libros de caballerías*, which were the pulp fiction of the day. This has been seen by some as evidence of a deep-seated cynicism, or at least an anti-romanticism, on Cervantes's part. Lord Byron, for instance, in his poem, *Don Juan*, complained that *Don Quixote* had illustrated that it was futile to attempt to "redress men's wrongs, and rather check than punish crimes" because Cervantes in his "too true tale" had "shown how all such efforts fail."

To paraphrase Byron's critique of *Don Quixote*, he says that the novel shows that the life of virtue, pursued by Quixote, is nothing but a facile and futile fantasy, signifying nothing, thereby turning the truths of reason, as embodied in Greek philosophy, into nonsense, making of Socrates a figure similar to Don Quixote himself, nothing but Wisdom's fool, one whose wisdom is mere foolishness. According to Byron, Cervantes had used *Don Quixote* to laugh scornfully at virtue, seducing us to laugh with him, thereby destroying the whole Spanish history of chivalry and shaking the very foundations of faith and reason. For Byron, therefore, *Don Quixote* is nothing less than an iconoclastic attack on civilisation itself. Strong words indeed. In similar, if not such strident fashion, the great Russian novelist Dostoyevsky recorded in his diary that *Don Quixote* was "the saddest book ever written," because "it is a story of disillusionment." And yet, in a letter to his niece, Dostoyevsky went much deeper, stating that "of all the beautiful individuals in Christian literature, one stands out as the most perfect, Don Quixote," adding by way of paradox that "he is beautiful only because he is ridiculous." He then gets to the mystical and mysterious heart of the novel:

"Wherever compassion toward ridiculed and ingenious beauty is presented, the reader's sympathy is aroused. The mystery of humor lies in this excitation of compassion."[2]

Dostoyevsky wrote these words as he was beginning to create the quixotic character of Prince Myshkin, the protagonist of his novel *The Idiot*, who is clearly inspired by Don Quixote and indeed modelled on him. Prince Myshkin's transparent goodness, his lack of guile, and his noble simplicity make him an object of ridicule in the eyes of the cynically worldly and yet evoke sympathy in those who admire his virtue and see something akin to wisdom in his innocence. It is for this reason that Sancho Panza, for all his own scepticism and jaded worldliness, is attracted to the "holy foolishness" of his master. Don Quixote "has nothing of the rogue in him," he says. "[O]n the contrary he could do no harm to anyone, but good to all, nor has he any malice in him; why, a child would convince him it is night at noonday, and it is on account of this simplicity that I love him as I love the cockles of my heart, and I can't invent a way of leaving him, no matter what piece of foolishness he does."[3]

It is, therefore, in this light, perhaps, that we should read *Don Quixote*, seeing its protagonist as a holy fool with whom we should sympathize, even when he is at his most ridiculous. And yet there is a real danger in taking this quixotic foolishness too far. If we are not careful, we begin to see the foolishness as something which is an end in itself, as a divine madness separating faith from reason. This is a perilous path to take, leading as it does into the quagmire of the heresy of fideism.

Don Quixote can lead us in this direction, seducing us to see irrational faith as preferable to rational disbelief, or it can lead us in the opposite direction, enticing us to believe that

2   F. M. Dostoyevsky, *Polnoe sobranie sochinenii*, Vol. 28–2 (Leningrad: Nauka, 1985), 251; quoted in *The New York Review of Books*, November 19, 1998.

3   Miguel de Cervantes, *Don Quixote* (New York, Signet Classic edition, 1964), 613.

all faith is an expression of madness, nothing but an irrational fantasy to be spurned and ridiculed. It is, however, clear that Cervantes intends to lead us in neither direction, both of which are inimical to the Catholic insistence on the intrinsic and indissoluble bond of faith and reason (*fides et ratio*). He leads us, in fact, to Don Quixote's conversion to the fullness of Catholic realism, philosophically understood, in which goodness is not married to madness, but in which sanctity and sanity are one and indivisible in the holy matrimony of *fides* with *ratio*. In short and in sum, Don Quixote is healed of his delusions at the end of the novel, regaining his sanity which finds full and final expression in his reconciliation with Holy Mother Church.

"Blessed be the Almighty for this great benefit He has granted me!" he cries in a loud voice upon awakening from sleep during his final illness. "Infinite are His mercies, and undiminished even by the sins of men."

"What mercies and what sins of men are you talking about?" asks his niece.

"Mercies," Don Quixote answers, "that God has just this moment granted to me in spite of all my sins. My judgment is now clear and unfettered, and that dark cloud of ignorance has disappeared, which the continual reading of those detestable books of knight-errantry had cast over my understanding. I find, dear niece, that my end approaches, but I would have it remembered that though in my life I was reputed a madman, yet in my death this opinion was not confirmed."

Coming to his senses, he asks for a priest to hear his confession. The priest, after absolving him of his sins, announces that there is no doubt that he is at the point of death, "and there is also no doubt that he is in his entire right mind."

"I was mad," Don Quixote says a little later, "but I am now in my senses."

In such a state of sound mind and in a state of grace, "after he had received all the sacraments," Don Quixote breathes his last.

And so this most enigmatic of novels concludes with the happiest of endings in which the madness of life is healed by the holiest of deaths. Let the final words belong to the words inscribed on Quixote's tomb:

> Here lies the noble fearless knight,
> Whose valor rose to such a height;
> When Death at last did strike him down,
> His was the victory and renown.
> He reck'd the world of little prize,
> And was a bugbear in men's eyes;
> But had the fortune in his age
> To live a fool and die a sage.[4]

On St. George's Day 1616, Miguel de Cervantes also breathed his last, on exactly the same day as the death of William Shakespeare. It was singularly and surely providentially appropriate that the brightest jewels in the golden ages of Spanish and English literature should have taken their respective last bows together. It was also singularly appropriate that these slayers of dragons should have died on the Feast of St. George, true knights as they were, who had wielded their pens like lances in the service of the good, the true, and the beautiful.

A POSTSCRIPT ON KNIGHT ERRANTRY

Considering Cervantes's evident disdain for chivalrous romances and books of knight errantry, it is important that we make the necessary distinction between the contemporary pulp fiction

---

4   Ibid., 1045–1049.

of the sixteenth century which Cervantes lampoons and the mediaeval works which were their source of inspiration. In the same manner in which Tolkien's epic, *The Lord of the Rings*, towers over the many contemporary works in the fantasy genre that it inspired, most of which are dire in the extreme, so mediaeval works, such as *The Song of Roland* and the *Poem of El Cid*, tower over the sixteenth-century romances which they inspired and which Cervantes scorns. Having fought against the forces of Islam at Lepanto, Cervantes would not have taken lightly those works of mediaeval literature that sang of the epic adventures of Christian heroes, such as Charlemagne, Roland, and El Cid, in the struggle against the Islamic powers that had conquered Spain and were threatening the rest of Europe.

In this context, and while we are discussing Spanish literature, it would be a sin of omission not to mention, albeit all too briefly, the *Poem of El Cid*, the anonymous Old Castilian epic that stands to the mediaeval French epic *The Song of Roland* as the *Odyssey* does to *The Iliad*. Whereas *The Song of Roland* tells of the historic battle of Roncevaux and Roland's heroic death in the doomed rear guard of Charlemagne's army, inviting and invoking parallels with the heroism of Hector or Achilles, the latter, the *Poem of El Cid*, transcribed from campfire ballads towards the end of the twelfth century, tells of the deeds of Rodrigo Diaz del Vivar in a manner that will remind its readers of the journeyings of Odysseus. A *caballero* from the country near Burgos, Diaz, the hero of the Reconquista of Spain, was exiled by his king for some questionable doings in the war against Spain's Muslim rulers. The poem that begins with his leaving home and wife—"like a nail pulled out of its flesh"—tells of his travels and travails, and of his long, weary fight to regain prosperity and be reunited to kith and kin. A veritable epic of honour and of love which interweaves family, friendship, fealty, and especially faith, it is, to be sure, a tale of doughty deeds told in rousing verse, which nobody, even Don Quixote, should fear to read.

10

The Metaphysical Poets

In the history of English literature a place of honour is held by the Metaphysical Poets, even though there is much disagreement with regard to what exactly is meant by the label and with regard to which poets deserve to have the label appended to them. Those poets usually labelled as metaphysical include John Donne, George Herbert, Robert Southwell, Andrew Marvell, Henry Vaughan, and Richard Crashaw. We will be looking at four of these: Donne, Herbert, Southwell, and Crashaw. Before we do so, let us take a look at what is normally meant by what is called Metaphysical Poetry.

Helen Gardner, one of the great scholars of the Metaphysical Poets, concentrates on the role of the conceit as the "most immediately striking feature" of metaphysical poetry. Her artfully succinct definition of the metaphysical conceit is worth quoting as a key that helps us understand the genre:

A conceit is a comparison whose ingenuity is more striking than its justness, or, at least, is more immediately striking. All comparisons discover likeness in things unlike: a comparison becomes a conceit when we are made to concede likeness while being strongly conscious of unlikeness. A brief comparison can be a conceit if two things patently unlike, or which we should never think of together, are shown to be alike in a single point in a single way, or in such a context, that we feel their incongruity. Here a conceit is like a spark made by striking two stones together. After the flash the stones are just two stones. Metaphysical poetry abounds in such flashes.[1]

Gardner's definition of "conceit" is remarkably similar to the Chestertonian understanding of "paradox," which can be defined as an apparent contradiction pointing to a deeper truth. The synonymous nature of the metaphysical *conceit* and the Chestertonian *paradox* becomes immediately apparent if the former word is replaced by the latter in the above passage. Indeed, the parallels between the use of the conceit by the Metaphysical Poets and the use of paradox by Chesterton are so striking that one feels that Chesterton should be redefined as a metaphysical novelist or as a metaphysical essayist. This parallel between Chestertonian prose and Metaphysical Poetry is even more apparent when we consider Gardner's exposition of the didactic dimension of metaphysical poetry that the employment of the conceit represents: "A metaphysical conceit . . . is not indulged in for its own sake. It is used . . . to persuade, or it is used to define, or to prove a point." And again:

In a metaphysical poem the conceits are instruments of definition in an argument or instruments to persuade. The poem has something to say which the conceit explicates or something to urge which the conceit helps to forward. . . . I have said that the first impression a conceit makes is of ingenuity rather than of justice: the metaphysical conceit aims at making us concede justness while admiring ingenuity.[2]

Having discussed the defining feature of Metaphysical Poetry, let us begin our brief survey of four of the Metaphysical Poets.

---

1 Helen Gardner, Introduction to *The Metaphysical Poets* (London: Penguin Classics edition, 1985), 19.
2 Ibid., 21.

The martyred Jesuit St. Robert Southwell is one of the greatest Englishmen in the whole of England's long and chequered history. A convert to the Faith who was forced into exile in order to study for the priesthood, Southwell returned to the shores of his homeland to minister in secret to England's outlawed Catholics. As with the other English Jesuit missionaries to England, Southwell knew that, if caught, he faced imprisonment, torture, and an excruciatingly slow death through being hanged, drawn, and quartered. He knew also that Queen Elizabeth's extensive spy network amongst the Catholic community made it very likely that he would be caught sooner or later. In the event, he eluded arrest for several years. During this time, he befriended Shakespeare's patron, the Earl of Southampton, becoming his confessor, and in all probability became a confidant of Shakespeare himself.

Whereas England's anti-Catholic propagandists condemned Southwell as a "traitor" and a "spy" in the service of Rome, he was to England's beleaguered Catholics a dashing and daring hero more akin to the Scarlet Pimpernel of later legend. The difference was that the Scarlet Pimpernel was a fictional hero during the Great Terror in France, whereas Robert Southwell was a real-life hero, one of "God's spies" during the earlier Terror in England.

Following his arrest in 1592, Southwell was tortured repeatedly and imprisoned for three years before facing gruesome execution. At the time of his death, his poetry was widely known and widely read, even by his enemies. He would influence many of the greatest poets in the English language, including Shakespeare, most notably, but also Michael Drayton, Edmund Spenser, John Donne, George Herbert, Richard Crashaw, and Gerard Manley Hopkins. More importantly, he was canonized in 1970 by Pope Paul VI as one of the Forty Martyrs of England and Wales.

Although Southwell's poetry is important in its own right, it is of added value because of its influence on Shakespeare who alludes to Southwell's poetry in several of his plays, particularly in *Romeo and Juliet, The Merchant of Venice, Hamlet,* and *King Lear.* Nowhere is this connection more evident than in the connection between Southwell's use of "God's spice" in one of his poems and Shakespeare's punning reference to it as "God's spies" in *King Lear.* Southwell's poem, "Decease Release," written in the first person with Mary Stuart, Queen of Scots, as the narrator, refers to the executed queen as "pounded spice":

> The pounded spice both taste and scent doth please,
>> In fading smoke the force doth incense show,
> The perished kernel springeth with increase,
>> The lopped tree doth best and soonest grow.
>
> God's spice I was and pounding was my due,
>> In fading breath my incense savored best,
> Death was the mean my kernel to renew,
>> By lopping shot I up to heavenly rest.

Although the poem is Southwell's tribute to the executed Queen of Scots, its being written in the first person gave it added potency following his own execution. Like the martyred queen of whom he wrote, Southwell was also "pounded spice" whose essence is more pleasing and valued for being crushed: "God's spice I was and pounding was my due." As a Jesuit in Elizabethan England, Southwell had been one of "God's spies," who, being caught, became "God's spice," ground to death that he might receive his martyr's reward in Heaven. "Upon such sacrifices," Shakespeare exclaims through the lips of Lear immediately after the punning reference to "God's spies," "the gods themselves throw incense."

John Donne was baptized as a Catholic and connected through his mother with St. Thomas More but switched his allegiance to the Anglican church when still a young man. Thereafter he commenced the writing of religious polemic against the Catholic Church. Yet he seems to have paid a high psychological price for his apostasy, evident in the dark satire and disturbed scepticism of "The Progress of the Soul" (1601), a work that exhibited a mind and heart in turmoil. It was not until his ordination into the Anglican ministry in 1614 that he acquired a sense of theological settlement and stability, though not without the occasional attacks of doubt. The poems of Donne that every Catholic should read would include his "Holy Sonnets" and also his longer poem "Good Friday, 1613: Riding Westward."

George Herbert was the son of Lady Magdalen Herbert, to whom Donne addressed his "Holy Sonnets." Like Donne, Herbert took Anglican orders. In both his life and works he represents the early flowering of that Anglo-Catholicism which was being championed in his day by William Laud. He died in the same year that Laud, later to be beheaded for endeavouring "to overthrow the Protestant religion," became Archbishop of Canterbury. Poems by George Herbert that should be on the reading list of every Catholic include "Easter," "The Agonie," "Vanitie," "Virtue," "The Pulley," and "Love."

Richard Crashaw, the son of a Puritan clergyman, converted to Catholicism during the English Civil War and was forced into exile. Living in abject poverty in Paris and then in Rome, he was eventually appointed, in April 1649, to the post of subcanon of the Cathedral of Loreto in Italy, dying only four months later. A devotee of St. Teresa of Avila, he is a poet of the stature of the great St. John of the Cross, that other great poet and follower of St. Teresa who also suffered greatly for the Faith. Many of Crashaw's shorter epigrammatic verses are truly delightful but his masterpiece is indubitably his "Hymn to the Name and Honour of the Admirable Saint Teresa."

11

Milton and Dryden

Two literary giants straddled the latter half of the seventeenth century, John Milton (1608–74) and John Dryden (1631–1700). It is to these giants that we shall now turn our attention.

Although almost all of the great writers prior to the mid-seventeenth century had been Catholic in either sympathy or practice, John Milton took up the Protestant cause with revolutionary zeal. Following the victory of Cromwell's Puritan army in the English Civil War, he supported and defended the execution of King Charles I. He was in the middle of writing *Paradise Lost* at the time of the Restoration of the monarchy, which he strongly opposed. Milton became so heterodox, denying the Trinity and the true divinity of Christ, that it is arguable that he cannot justifiably be called a Protestant or even a Christian of any sort in the true sense of the word. And yet Paradise Lost is indubitably one of the true masterpieces of world literature, following in the noble epic tradition of Homer and Virgil. As such, it should be read and enjoyed and appreciated by Catholics.

Nonetheless, Catholic readers of Milton's epic need to be aware of the heterodoxy that animates it. This heterodoxy will be our focus, therefore, even though such a critique should not blind us to the glorious sweep of Milton's use of the English language, or his gifts as a storyteller, or his wonderful depiction of marital love in the pre-lapsarian Garden.

At the dark heart of *Paradise Lost* is the looming and alluring presence of Milton's Satan, whose powerfully portrayed characterization has elicited sympathy from many readers of the poem, from Percy Shelley's eulogizing of him in the early nineteenth century to modern manifestations of sympathy for him in our own time. With respect to the latter, Edward Simon, in an article for *The Atlantic* on March 16, 2017, tries to get to grips with the fascination that Americans feel for the character of Lucifer in Milton's epic. In a well-written and well-reasoned article, Simon sees aspects of Milton's Satan in the characterization of thoroughly modern anti-heroes in contemporary TV dramas, especially *The Sopranos*, *Mad Men*, and *Breaking Bad*, all of which are seen to reflect in some manner the American dream. This morbid fascination with Milton's archetypal anti-hero prompts Simon to ask a provocative question: What's so "American" about John Milton's Lucifer?

There is, however, another provocative question that must be asked if we are to avoid misunderstanding and misconstruing Milton's Satan. Regardless of how "American" he is, we need to ask how Christian he is.

At the heart of such a question is a paradox. From an orthodox Christian perspective, the real Satan is, at one and the same time, a Christian and an anti-Christian. He is a Christian in the sense that he knows that Christ is the Incarnate Son of God; he is an anti-Christian because he hates the Son as he hates the Father. He knows the Trinitarian God, and he hates him. He is not an unbeliever. He is a rebel who is at war with the reality in which he has no choice but to believe.

The demons in the Gospel do not deny the authority of Christ. They defy him, as far as they are able, and despise him, but they do not and cannot deny him. We see the same paradox in the manner in which Dracula, in the old movies, recoils in horror from the sight of a crucifix. He hates the symbol of the power of Christ, but he cannot help but retreat from it because the power he despises is real.

The problem with Milton's Lucifer is that he is not synonymous with the Lucifer of the Bible or the Lucifer of Christian tradition. He is a figment of Milton's heterodox imagination. Milton's God is not the Trinitarian God of the Christians but a Unitarian God whose Son is a mere creature, albeit the greatest of all creatures. Considering Milton's theological break with orthodoxy, his denial of the Trinity and, in consequence, his denial of the Incarnation also, it is grievously erroneous to see *Paradise Lost* as a Christian work. Except for its biblical trappings, it is no more Christian, in an orthodox sense, than the earlier epics of Homer and Virgil, and arguably less so. It might be argued, for instance, as we have done, that Homer and Virgil were groping in the right direction, towards the light of the Gospel, whereas Milton, rejecting the Church and the traditions of Christendom, was groping in the wrong direction, away from the light of the Gospel.

William Blake might have been right when he said of Milton that he was "of the devil's party without knowing it." Certainly Milton was doing the real devil a service in inventing a mythical devil who has proved so attractive. Milton's Lucifer has what he perceives to be a just grievance and rebels against the perceived injustice with great courage. By way of contrast, it is hard to feel much sympathy with Milton's God who is not loved because he is not loveable. He is an omnipotent Puritan prig who is right because of his might. A Pharisee himself, he might well have been the sort of God whom the Pharisees worshipped, but he has little in common with the God of the Christians. Meanwhile, Milton's Son is not worshipped because he is not God. In marked contrast to the biblical Jesus, he is depicted by Milton as a warrior who boasts of his martial prowess. Perhaps nobody in history has done more to evoke sympathy for the devil than John Milton, even though we may presume that he would have been appalled at this dark side of his legacy.

In answer to the original provocative question, Milton's Lucifer is not Christian. He is no more Christian than the poet who gave him life. In consequence, those who feel that they have sympathy for the Miltonian devil are not sympathizing with the real Satan, any more than they are rebelling against the real Christ.

Having no doubt stirred up a good deal of controversy, and having broken ranks with those many champions of Milton, such as C. S. Lewis, in highlighting the poet's heterodoxy over his indubitable genius, we will move on hastily to less contentious territory.[1]

The other literary giant of the latter half of the seventeenth century whom Catholics should know is John Dryden, whose greatest work, *The Hind and the Panther*, published in 1687, two years after his conversion to Catholicism, is a monumental *apologia* for the Catholic Faith and an equally monumental rebuttal of the claims of Anglicanism. Like Crashaw, Dryden is a true colossus whose neglect by the modern world is scandalous. He deserves, like Crashaw, to become much better known.

Like so many of his contemporaries, Dryden was buffeted by the religious conflicts that plagued the seventeenth century. His family had been staunch Parliamentarians during the English Civil War and his cousin, Sir Gilbert Pickering, was Cromwell's chamberlain, a fact which worked to the young Dryden's advantage when he came to London in 1657. His

---

1   Those wishing to examine the case for Milton's defence should read C. S. Lewis's *Preface to Paradise Lost*, especially chapter XII. Space precludes engagement with it here. The present author finds Lewis's arguments unconvincing.

Heroic Stanzas on Cromwell's death in 1658 marked the beginning of his literary career.

Having begun with Puritan sympathies, Dryden modified his religious position over the years. His didactic poem, *Religio Laici*, published in 1682, argued the case for Anglicanism. His finest poem, *The Hind and the Panther*, published five years later, heralded his conversion to Catholicism. Since his conversion coincided with the ascension to the throne of the avowedly Catholic James II, many have suspected that he had cynical and self-serving motives in converting at this time, but the fact that he did not revert to the established Church when the Protestant William III usurped the throne in 1688 suggests otherwise. Certainly *The Hind and the Panther*, which is the one poem by Dryden that every Catholic should know, bears the hallmarks of a genuine *apologia* for the Catholic Faith and for the poet's embrace of it. It is a formal allegory in which the Hind (a personification of the Catholic Church) is in dialogue with the Panther (a personification of the Anglican Church). Divided into three parts, the first part deals with the various religious denominations in contemporary England, the most eminent of which is the Hind, described as "milk-white immortal and unchanged." The second part tackles contentious doctrinal issues associated with church authority and the dogma of transubstantiation. The final part calls for an alliance between the Crown, the Anglican Church, and the Catholic Church to counter the rise of the various Protestant sects.

Although *The Hind and the Panther* was attacked venomously and vociferously for its Catholicism by contemporary critics, which is not surprising considering the very anti-Catholic times in which it was written, later generations of critics, including some truly great writers, lavished praise upon it. Among its admirers were Alexander Pope, Samuel Johnson, Sir Walter Scott, and William Hazlitt. Even Lord Macaulay, who had no sympathy whatsoever for Dryden's Catholicism, described some of the passages in the poem as "magnificent."

Considering the praise bestowed upon *The Hind and the Panther* by some of the *eminenti* of English letters, we might hope that in healthier and happier times this magnificent poem and the reputation of its equally magnificent author might rise from the ashes of neglect like a phoenix of faith, resurrected and born again within the hearts of new generations of civilised readers.

12

The Romantic Poets

William Blake, William Wordsworth, and Samuel Taylor Coleridge are sometimes called the early Romantic poets in recognition of their pioneering role in English romanticism and as a means of distinguishing them from the second generation of Romantic poets, of which the most prominent were Lord Byron, Percy Bysshe Shelley, and John Keats. In order to understand the importance of these tremendously influential poets, we need to know something about romanticism itself. What is romanticism? Is it right or wrong? Is it right or left? Is it revolutionary or reactionary? What *is* it? Such questions are not academic, nor are they unimportant. On the contrary, they help us to understand the world in which we live.

In the "Afterword" to the third edition of *The Pilgrim's Regress*, C. S. Lewis complained that "romanticism" had acquired so many different meanings that, as a word, it had become meaningless. "I would not now use this word . . . to describe anything," he complained, "for I now believe it to be a word of such varying senses that it has become useless and should be banished from our vocabulary." Begging to differ with Lewis, if we banished words because they have multifarious meanings or because their meaning is abused or debased by maladroit malapropism, we should soon find it impossible to say anything at all. Take, for example, the word "love." Few words are more abused, yet few words are more necessary to an understanding of ourselves. John Lennon and Jesus Christ did not have the same thing in mind when they spoke of love. C. S. Lewis understood this, of course. He understood it so well that he wrote a whole book on the subject. In *The Four Loves* he sought to *define* "love." And what is true of a word such as "love" is equally true of a word like "romanticism." If we are to advance in understanding, we must abandon the notion of abolishing the word and commence instead with a definition of our terms. Lewis, in spite of his protestations, also understood this truth and proceeded from his plaintive call for the abolition of the word to the enumeration of various definitions of it, claiming that "we can distinguish at least seven kinds of things which are called 'romantic.'" From four loves to seven romanticisms, Lewis was not about to abandon meaning, or the *mens sana*, to men without minds or chests.

Since Lewis's seven separate definitions of romanticism are a little unwieldy, it is necessary to hone our definition of romanticism into an encompassing unity within which the other definitions can be said to subsist. What makes romanticism distinct; or, to return to our initial question, what *is* it? According to the *Collins Dictionary of Philosophy*, romanticism is "a style of thinking and looking at the world that dominated nineteenth-century Europe." Arising in early mediaeval culture, it referred originally to tales in the Romance language about courtly love and other sentimental topics, as distinct from works in classical Latin. From the beginning, therefore, "romanticism" stood in contra-distinction to "classicism." The former referred to an outlook marked by refined and responsive *feelings* and thus could be said to be inward-looking, subjective, "sensitive," and given to noble dreams; the latter is marked by empiricism, governed by science and precise measures, and could be said to be outward-looking, or objective.

Having defined our terms, albeit in the broadest and most sweeping sense, we can proceed to a discussion of the ways in which human society has oscillated between the two alternative visions of reality represented by classicism and romanticism. First, however, we must insist that the oscillation is itself an aberration. It is a product of modernity. In the middle ages there was no such oscillation between these two extremes of perception. On the contrary, the mediaeval world was characterized by, indeed it was defined by, a theological and philosophical unity which transcended the division between romanticism and classicism. The nexus of philosophy and theology in the Platonic-Augustinian and Aristotelian-Thomistic view of man represented the fusion of *fides et ratio*, the uniting of faith and reason. Take, for example, the use of the figurative or the allegorical in mediaeval literature, or the use of symbolism in mediaeval art. The function of the figurative in mediaeval art and literature was not intended primarily to arouse spontaneous *feelings* in the observer or reader, but to encourage the observer or reader to see the philosophical or theological significance beneath the symbolic configuration. In this sense, mediaeval art, informed by mediaeval philosophy and theology, is much more objective and outward-looking than the most "realistic" examples of modern art. The former points to abstract ideas which are the fruits of a philosophical tradition existing independently of either the artist or the observer; the latter derives its "realism" solely from the feelings and emotions of those "experiencing" it. One demands that the artist and the observer reach beyond themselves to the transcendent truth that is out there; the other recedes into the transient feelings of subjective experience. The surrender of the transcendental to the transient, the perennial to the ephemeral, is the mark of post-Christian and post-rational society. It is also a consequence of the triumph of the subjectivism of a certain type of romanticism.

With respect to the way in which romanticism manifested itself in English literature, we can say that it represented a reaffirmation of the importance of human feeling as a reaction against the cold empiricism and philosophical materialism of the eighteenth-century Enlightenment. This romantic reaction in England could be said to have had its genesis in 1798 with the publication of *Lyrical Ballads* by Wordsworth and Coleridge. Published shortly after the French Revolution, the poems in *Lyrical Ballads* represented the poets' recoil from the rationalism that had led to the Reign of Terror that followed in the Revolution's wake. Wordsworth would pass beyond the "serene and blessed mood" of optimistic pantheism displayed in his "Lines Composed a Few Miles above Tintern Abbey" to a full embrace of Anglican Christianity as exhibited in the allegorical depiction of Christ in "Resolution and Independence." Coleridge threw down the allegorical gauntlet of Christianity in "The Rime of the Ancient Mariner," and in his "Hymn before Sunrise in the Vale of Chamouni" he saw beyond majestic nature (*O Sovran Blanc!*) to the majesty of the God of nature:

> Who made you glorious as the Gates of Heaven
> Beneath the keen full moon? Who bade the sun
> Clothe you with rainbows? Who, with living flowers
> Of loveliest blue, spread garlands at your feet?
> God! let the torrents, like a shout of nations,
> Answer! and let the ice-plains echo, God!
> God! sing ye meadow-streams with gladsome voice!
> Ye pine-groves, with your soft and soul-like sounds!
> And they too have a voice, yon piles of snow,
> And in their perilous fall shall thunder, God!

If Wordsworth and Coleridge, in their reaction against the Enlightenment, had rediscovered the purity and passion of Christianity, the other great Romantic Poet, William Blake, in his own quixotically eccentric way, was also reacting against the Enlightenment, lamenting the "dark satanic mills" of industrialism. Although he shared the desire of Wordsworth and Coleridge for a purer vision untainted by Enlightenment rationalism, his dabbling in theology was singularly peculiar and ultimately heterodox, which is not to say that his wonderful poetry is not worth reading.

The pattern of reaction initiated by the first wave of Romantic Poets would be repeated in the various manifestations of neo-mediaevalism that would follow in its wake and which were a consequence of its influence. The Gothic Revival, heralded by the architect Augustus Pugin in the 1830s, and championed by the art critic John Ruskin twenty years later, sought to discover a purer aesthetic through a return to mediaeval notions of beauty. The Oxford Movement, spearheaded by John Henry Newman, Edward Pusey, and John Keble, sought a return to a purer Catholic vision for the Church of England, leapfrogging the Reformation in an attempt to graft the Victorian Anglican Church onto the Catholic Church of mediaeval England through the promotion of Catholic liturgy and a Catholic understanding of ecclesiology and the sacraments. The pre-Raphaelite Brotherhood, formed sometime around 1850 by Dante Gabriel Rossetti, John Everett Millais, William Holman Hunt, and others, sought a purer vision of art by leapfrogging the art of the Late Renaissance in pursuit of the clarity of mediaeval and Early Renaissance painting which existed, so the pre-Raphaelites believed and as their name implied, prior to the innovations of Raphael.

Although these manifestations of romantic neo-mediaevalism transformed nineteenth-century culture, countering the optimistic and triumphalistic scientism of the Victorian imperial psyche, it would be wrong to imply that romanticism always led to mediaevalism. The neo-mediaeval tendencies of what might be termed light romanticism were paralleled by a dark romanticism, epitomized by the life and work of Byron and Shelley, which tended towards subjectivism and introspective self-indulgence.

If Wordsworth and Coleridge were reacting against the rationalist iconoclasm of the French Revolution, Byron and Shelley seemed to be reacting against Wordsworth's and Coleridge's reaction. Greatly influenced by *Lyrical Ballads*, Byron and Shelley were nonetheless uncomfortable at the Christian traditionalism that Wordsworth and Coleridge began to embrace. Byron devoted a great deal of the Preface to *Childe Harold's Pilgrimage* to attacking the "monstrous mummeries of the middle ages," and Shelley, in his "Defence of Poetry," anathematized Tradition by insisting that poets were slaves to the *zeitgeist* and that they were "the mirrors of the gigantic shadows which futurity casts upon the present." Slaves of the spirit of the Present, and mirrors of the giant presence of the Future, poets were warriors of Progress intent on vanquishing the superstitious remnants of Tradition. Perhaps these iconoclastic musings could be seen as transient youthful idealism, especially as there appeared to be signs that Byron yearned for something more solid than the inarticulate creedless deism espoused in "The Prayer of Nature," and signs also that Shelley's militant atheism was softening into skylarking pantheism. Their early deaths, and the early death of their confrère, Keats, has preserved them forever as icons of Youth whose poetry often attained heights of beauty and perception which transcended the incoherence of their philosophy.

The Byronic aura of the second generation of romantics crossed the channel and metamorphosed into the Decadence of Baudelaire, Verlaine, and Huysmans, all of whom plumbed the depths of despair before recoiling in horror into the arms of the Catholic Church. The symbolism of the French Decadence re-crossed the Channel under the patronage of Oscar Wilde, who was an aficionado of Baudelaire, Verlaine, and Huysmans. From the publication of *Lyrical Ballads* in 1798 to the death of Oscar Wilde in 1900, romanticism could be seen, in large part, to be a reaction against the rationalism of the Enlightenment. It was, however, schizophrenic. The "light" romanticism of Wordsworth and Coleridge staggered falteringly in the direction of a revitalized Christianity; the "dark" romanticism of Byron, Shelley, and Keats led eventually to subjectivism, nihilism, and postmodernism.

Let us conclude by returning to our original questions. What is romanticism? At its best, it is the generally healthy reaction of the heart to the hardness of the head. Is it right or wrong? It is often brilliantly right and sometimes disastrously wrong. Is it right or left? It is neither, defying all efforts to be classified thus. Is it revolutionary or reactionary? It depends, of course, on how we are defining our terms. If, however, we are referring to political revolutions of the ilk of 1789 and 1917, then it is counter-revolutionary and reactionary, at least in its English manifestation. What *is* it? It is, at its best, an effort to rediscover what has been lost, a groping in the depths of experience and in the darkness of modernity for the light of truth that tradition preserves.

13

Feminine Genius:
Jane Austen, Mary Shelley,
and the Brontë Sisters

For the most part, prior to the nineteenth century, women were largely absent from among the literary *eminenti*. Since then, they have been well represented. We will focus on those women writers from the early nineteenth century whose feminine genius blazed a trail for future generations.

JANE AUSTEN

Jane Austen is more than a giantess among women writers. She is also a giantess among the giants, holding a place of pride and prominence among the greatest writers of either sex and of all ages. She does not merely tower above George Eliot, Mary Shelley, Virginia Woolf, and the Brontë sisters, she also towers above almost every male writer. There are indeed relatively few writers in the whole history of literature that tower above her. One thinks of Homer and Virgil, Dante and Shakespeare, but beyond these edifices she holds her own among the greatest of all time. She can be mentioned in the same breath as Tolstoy, Dostoyevsky, and Dickens. Few indeed can hold a candle to her in terms of the sheer brilliance of her work and the perceptive depths that she fathoms.

Like Shakespeare, Jane Austen can be said to be not of an age but for all time, and yet, as with Shakespeare, it helps to know something of the age in which she wrote in order to understand the fullness of what she is saying in her work. Shakespeare was almost certainly a believing Catholic living in anti-Catholic times; knowing this about him helps us to understand the subplots of *The Merchant of Venice* and *Hamlet*, and the angst and anger that animates *Macbeth*, *King Lear*, and *Othello*. Similarly, knowing that Jane Austen was a devout Christian living in an age in which romanticism was at war with faithless rationalism helps us understand her way of seeing the world and the ideas that were shaping it. This being so, let us look at the lady and her age.

Born in 1775, Miss Austen entered a world which was ripe for, and would soon be rife with, revolution. The American Revolution was ushering into existence a new sort of nation, bereft of both monarchy and aristocracy, and enshrining in its Constitution the principles of the Enlightenment. Then, in 1789, the French Revolution brought down the *ancien régime*, replacing it with a secularist tyranny, the darkness and terror of which laid the ideological foundations for future communist tyrannies. Against these new ideas Edmund Burke sounded a sagacious and cautionary note, especially in his *Reflections on the Revolution in France*, which was published at the end of 1790, when Jane Austen was fifteen. Many of Burke's views can be seen to be represented in the character of Fanny Price in *Mansfield Park*, suggestive of Austen's own sympathy for Burke's anti-revolutionary position, and it might be suggested that the hero's name, Edmund Bertram, is a phonetic allusion to Edmund Burke himself, which would perhaps indicate that Burke had been a mentor to the young Miss Austen as Bertram had been a mentor to the young Miss Price.

Perhaps the most frequently recurring theme in Austen's work is a disdain for the irrational tenets of romanticism, which emphasized emotion and the feelings of the heart over the reasoning of the head. From her earliest juvenile writings, such as *Love and Freindship* (*sic*), written in 1790, to her mature novels of more than twenty years later, she lampoons the sort of romantic novels in which women are depicted as irrational beings, weak-willed and weak-minded. Whereas her own novels contain such women, who commit the folly of following feeling in defiance of the demands of moral responsibility, her heroines attain the fullness of human dignity, subjecting themselves as eminently rational creatures to the goodness of virtue and the objectivity of truth. In this, she has been called an Aristotelian, quite correctly, but she could as easily be described as a Thomist insofar as she accepted and embraced Christian realism in an age of embryonic relativism. She is, therefore, a veritable giantess as a philosopher, in addition to her genius as a storyteller and her perspicacity as an observer of the human condition.

As for Jane Austen's stance with respect to the Catholic Church, she was, like Burke, sympathetic to Catholicism at a time when anti-Catholic bigotry and sectarianism was the default position in English culture. Although this can be discerned implicitly in her novels, it was present most obviously and emphatically in her juvenilia, especially in the "History of England," which was written in 1791 when she was only fifteen-years-old. This "History" lampoons and satirizes the anti-Catholic stance of conventional history books, especially Oliver Goldsmith's outrageously "anti-papist" four-volume "history" of England. In stark and remarkable contrast to the bias of Protestant history that overlooked the tyranny of Tudor England, the teenage Miss Austen depicts Elizabeth I as an unmitigated tyrant and shows Mary, Queen of Scots to be the martyred victim of Tudor tyranny. In supporting the Catholic Stuarts against the anti-Catholic Tudors, she was countering the pride and prejudice of her times and was showing herself to be an unwitting prophet of what would later become known as Anglo-Catholicism. In this, as in so much else, Catholics can feel entirely comfortable in the presence of the feminine genius of Jane Austen.

MARY SHELLEY

Mary Shelley's *Frankenstein* is a work which, for all its flaws, continues to grip the popular imagination. What is it about this novel, written by a teenage girl two hundred years ago, that continues to fascinate us?

Is the secret of *Frankenstein*'s success its grappling with perennial questions about the relationship between scientific knowledge and moral philosophy? Is it still alive because it wrestles with fundamental questions of life and death? Is it larger than life because it grapples with the culture of death?

We could say so much about the influences that were working on Mary Shelley's young mind as she wrote the book. There is the looming presence of Milton, and, to a lesser degree, Dante. There is, moreover, the shadow of Percy Shelley's controversial sympathy for Milton's Satan, a romantic spin on Milton's epic which adds a darker shade of gloom to the spirit of rebellion haunting the novel's pages. More beguiling and enigmatic is Percy Shelley's own looming presence and hints of Mary's rebellion against it, the novel suggesting the wife's struggle to emerge from her husband's shadow—into a light to which he was hostile. There is the influence of Mary's father, the philosopher William Godwin, whose atheism is questioned by Mary in the questions that the novel asks. There is the confused and confusing influence of Jean-Jacques Rousseau and his idiotic flirtation with the chimeric idea of the Noble Savage.

Most fascinating, perhaps, is Mary's evident sympathy for the "light" romanticism of Coleridge and Wordsworth, as personified in the noble character of Henry Clerval and as alluded to intertextually throughout the novel, a sympathy that placed her at odds with the "dark" romanticism of her husband and his friend, Lord Byron. The romanticism of the light, epitomized by the works of Coleridge and Wordsworth, is rooted in the humility that leads to wonder and ultimately to the contemplation of beauty as a manifestation of God's presence in Creation. The romanticism of the dark, on the other hand, is rooted in the Byronic pride that seeks meaning egocentrically and introspectively, as something subjective to the self and therefore ultimately self-obsessive and narcissistic. This being so, it is intriguing that the teenage bride of Percy Shelley should contrast the self-obsessed and Byronically brooding Frankenstein with the selfless and Coleridgean figure of Clerval, the former being the sick and deluded villain and the latter his healthy alter ego.

What does this have to say about the mind of the teenage girl who wrote the novel? What was she experiencing during the eleven months in which the novel was being written? Might the darkness of her life shed light on the battle between the darkness and the light in *Frankenstein*? Is she perhaps present autobiographically within the novel, her tormented persona daubed across its pages in lurid shades of angst-driven self-expression? Does she haunt its pages like a restless ghost, seeking an elusive peace?

Mary began writing *Frankenstein* in June 1816, when she was still only eighteen, and would not finish it until the following May. The eleven months during which she was working on the novel were almost as macabre in real life as was the unfolding of the plot in her fevered imagination. In October 1816, Fanny Imlay, Mary's half-sister, committed suicide, and in December the drowned body of Harriet Shelley, the wife whom Shelley had deserted in order to elope with Mary, was discovered in the Serpentine, in London's

Hyde Park, some weeks after she had presumably committed suicide. On December 30, barely days after the discovery of Harriet's body, Mary and Percy were married. In March 1817, Percy was denied custody of the two children Harriet had borne. All this happened while Mary was working on *Frankenstein* and the shadow of these events account, no doubt, for much of the doom-laden and death-darkened atmosphere of the novel. It might almost be said, or at least plausibly suggested, that the ghost of Harriet Shelley haunted the author's imagination as she worked; if so, it is equally plausible to suggest that the Monster can be seen as a metaphor for the destructive power of the unleashed passion between Mary and Percy. This understanding of the subliminal depths of the novel would place Percy Shelley in the role of Frankenstein, his monstrous and self-obsessive ego leading to the death of his innocent wife, Harriet, as Frankenstein's egocentrism had led to the death of his innocent wife, Elizabeth. If this is so, we might see Mary Shelley, Shelley's second wife, as the Bride of Frankenstein, a teenage girl, caught in the grip of a monstrous culture of death, screaming in the vortex for some sense and semblance of light and life.

EMILY BRONTË

We will begin our discussion of the Brontë sisters with a confession and an apology. The confession is that we will not be considering two of the sisters, Charlotte and Anne, though both and especially the former warrant our attention. The apology is for the sin of omission that the neglect of these two sisters, and especially of Charlotte Brontë's *Jane Eyre*, represents. The excuse for this faux pas is the necessity of brevity occasioned by the space constraints of a book of this nature. In short and in sum, it is simply not possible to cover every work that warrants inclusion, rendering some sins of omission inevitable and unavoidable.

The confession and apology having been made, let us proceed to our discussion of Emily Brontë's novel, *Wuthering Heights*.

Emily Brontë seems to have been a home-loving daughter of a clergyman who lived chastely until the end of her days. Since this is the case, we find ourselves puzzled perhaps by the darkness and passion of her novel. How can one seemingly so innocuous create something seemingly so monstrous? How can an apparently prim and proper parson's daughter have created a Heathcliff and a Catherine?

In *Wuthering Heights*, we are confronted, uncomfortably, with unflinching cruelty, which, in the apparent absence of a benevolent God, seems to be meaningless. The suffering running rampant through the length and breadth of the novel is caused not only by the cruelty inflicted by the wickedness of the characters but by the lack of forgiveness and the desire for revenge. The innocent do not forgive the cruelty inflicted on them but become wicked themselves, destroying the innocence of others. The result is a destructive chain reaction in which more and more innocent lambs are turned into vengeful wolves. This is the very animus of the novel and the impetus of its plot. The absence of forgiveness is the very root of the evil that afflicts its characters. Thus, paradoxically, the very absence of Christian morality is the *invisible* moral presence that animates the action of the whole work. It is the scream in the vacuum created by virtue's neglect which causes us to hunger for its presence, much as a suffocating man craves for life-giving oxygen.

As for the *visible* moral presence of Christianity, it is seen most clearly in the words and actions of Nelly Dean, who attempts to bring the plot's protagonists to their senses. She reprimands Heathcliff for grieving Catherine, warning him that "[p]roud people breed sad sorrows for themselves." One wonders whether Heathcliff carries these words with him as the story unfolds, whether indeed he carries them with him to the grave. Either way, it is clear that Emily Brontë intends that we, the readers, take them with us as the plot unfolds before us. The whole story is the weaving of the sad sorrows brought upon the main protagonists by their own pride.

The wisdom of Nelly's words, and the suspicion that they are the words of the author speaking vicariously through her, are more apparent than ever in an exchange of words with Catherine, during which Nelly emerges as an incisive theologian.

"If I were in heaven, Nelly," says Catherine, "I should be extremely miserable."

"Because you are not fit to go there," Nelly answers. "All sinners would be miserable in heaven."

In the well-known passage that follows this exchange, probably the most-quoted but least-understood passage in the whole work, Catherine confesses the infernal nature of her "love" for Heathcliff. Heathcliff is not merely an idol, he is Catherine's god. She not only worships him, she is possessed by him. This demonic dimension was not lost on G. K. Chesterton, who wrote that Heathcliff "fails as a man as catastrophically as he succeeds as a demon."[1] The demonic is further suggested by the fact that Catherine's words, "I *am* Heathcliff," echo those of Milton's Satan, "myself am hell." Like Satan she is exiled from Heaven because everywhere, even Heaven, would be "a mighty stranger" to her if Heathcliff were not there; she would "not seem a part of it." She would rather be with him in Hell than without him in Heaven. Nothing will separate her from the "love" of her god, not even the love of God himself. She will be with Heathcliff forever, not merely "till death do us part" but beyond death itself. Heathcliff is the "eternal rock" upon which she builds her church. He is "a source of little visible delight" but, on the contrary, is "darkness visible," like Milton's Satan, and the source of all her suffering. Yet she will not be separated from the Hell she has chosen. She gets what she chooses. The angels in her dream who expel her from Heaven

---

1   G. K. Chesterton, *The Victorian Age in Literature* (London: Williams and Norgate, 1913), 113.

merely give her what she desires. Again, and to reiterate, this is profoundly orthodox Christian theology, in the finest tradition of Dante's *Inferno*.

As for Heathcliff, he is the disfigured figment of Emily's luridly vivid imagination, inspired in all probability by the disfigured figment of another female novelist's lurid imagination, Mary Shelley's Monster. Heathcliff wreaks and reaps havoc and destruction but, as with Mary Shelley's creature, he is also "demoniacal." He is physically monstrous and spiritually demonic at one and the same time, a devil incarnate. The parallels between Emily Brontë's monster/ demon and Mary Shelley's "demoniacal" creature are significant and show a certain kinship of spirit between the two novelists. Whereas Mary Shelley can be seen as *groping* towards traditional Christian morality *in spite* of her anti-Christian upbringing, Emily Brontë can be seen to be *grasping* the same morality *because* of her upbringing. One is in the dark groping for the light, the other is in the light but showing us what it is like to be in the dark. If there is one significant difference in their respective approaches, it springs from the influence of Milton's heterodox musings on Shelley, and the confusion it causes to her moral vision, as opposed to the evident influence of Dante's profoundly orthodox Muse on the work of Emily, and the clarity that springs from it.

The novel ends on a light note, in both senses of the word. The darkness lifts and the emergent light lightens the burden of evil that has loomed, doom-laden, over the whole work. Heathcliff is dead. The demon has departed. Wuthering Heights is free of its malevolent master. His death is, therefore, an exorcism. Happiness was not possible in his presence. It is the removal of the evil that allows the good to flourish in the novel's final hope-filled pages.

14

The Muse Betrothed: Manzoni

If the great masterpiece of Italian literature, Dante's *Divine Comedy*, could realistically be acclaimed as the greatest poem ever written, the other great masterpiece of Italian literature, *The Betrothed* (*I Promessi Sposi*) by Alessandro Manzoni, could be acclaimed as the greatest novel. This latter claim will come as a surprise to those who might not even have heard of Manzoni's classic work. And yet, in spite of the neglect it has suffered, it rivals *Don Quixote*, *Pride and Prejudice*, *A Tale of Two Cities*, *War and Peace*, *The Brothers Karamazov*, and any other claimants to literary preeminence. Such an appraisal of its merit would certainly accord with the view of most Italians who are baffled by the relative lack of recognition that Manzoni's *magnum opus* has received globally. It forms an indispensable part of the curriculum in Italian high schools and Manzoni's embrace of the Florentine dialect in his writing of *The Betrothed* helped to establish and formalize the modern Italian language. Furthermore, as a work that is more accessible than *The Divine Comedy*, it is the most widely read of all works of Italian literature and, with the exception of Dante's *Commedia*, the most widely critiqued and scrutinized by scholars.

Alessandro Manzoni was a revert to the practice of the Catholic Faith, having wandered off as a young man in pursuit of the fashionable and anti-Catholic secularism espoused by the followers of Voltaire. Having returned to the Catholic Faith with a renewed vigour and fervour, he began writing religious poetry and authored a scholarly treatise on Catholic morality. It was, therefore, as a devout Catholic that Manzoni set to work on *The Betrothed*, his own muse being betrothed to the essential truths that the novel shines forth.

First published in 1827 and later, in 1842, in a revised definitive version, *The Betrothed* is an historical novel recounting events from two centuries earlier. At the heart of the story is the agonizing relationship of Renzo and Lucia, the betrothed couple, who are swept apart by political intrigue and circumstance. It follows the hapless pair in their seemingly hopeless quest to be reunited, a storyline which will remind American readers of Longfellow's *Evangeline*. Against the backdrop of petty tyranny and political turmoil and amidst the mayhem of revolutionary mobs and the miasma of plague-ridden streets, the story of the lovers is interwoven with the stories of great sinners and even greater saints. Its greatest strength, however, is the menagerie of multifarious characters that Manzoni presents to the reader, a motley medley of all that is best and worst in humanity, much as Chaucer presents to the reader in the General Prologue to the *Canterbury Tales*. A brief depiction of the most important of these will provide a picture, a character portrait, of the novel itself.

Lucia is a worthy heroine in the tradition of great literary heroines. She reminds us of Homer's Penelope in her faithful fortitude in the midst of great trials and tribulations, exhibiting saintly spiritual strength in the very heart of the darkness in which she all too often finds herself. Like Penelope, she is besieged by the unwelcome advances of wicked men and beset by troubles which are not of her own making. She exhibits the powerful silence of Shakespeare's Cordelia in her resolve to refrain from the path of least resistance, retaining her virtue in the midst of viciousness. In so doing she also reminds us of Dante's Beatrice insofar as she represents a very icon of idealized femininity, worthy of anyone's love and warranting great sacrifice on the part of the lover in the quest to win her hand.

Renzo is utterly unworthy of her. He is hot-headed, rash in his judgments, and rushed in his actions. His lack of prudence and temperance all too often makes matters worse. And yet, in spite of his weaknesses, he is good and stout-hearted, and is lacking in neither courage nor cunning. For this reason, the reader cannot help liking him, in spite of his infuriating lack of judgment. We wish him well and wish him success in being reunited with the woman of whom he is so evidently the inferior.

In Don Abbondio and Fra Cristoforo we are shown the worst and the best in the priesthood and the religious life, much as Chaucer shows us the worst and the best in presenting us with the Friar and the Parson. Don Abbondio is craven in his abandonment of Renzo and Lucia to the wickedness of Don Rodrigo, placing his own self-interest and material comfort over the good of his flock. In contrast, Fra Cristoforo is fearless in his pursuit of justice for the betrothed couple, striding into the very lion's den in order to confront Don Rodrigo.

In Don Rodrigo and the Unnamed (*L'Innominato*), Manzoni presents us with two fearsome tyrants, each of whom has tyrannized the weak in the wielding of power for his own self-serving purposes. In the latter, he also shows us one of the most powerful and palpable examples of spiritual conversion in all of literature, a conversion which was based on the real-life conversion of Francesco Bernardino Visconti.

Two other characters based upon real-life historical figures are Federico Borromeo and the Nun of Monza, the former a cousin of St. Charles Borromeo who followed his kinsman as Cardinal Archbishop of Milan, as well as following in his kinsman's saintly footsteps as a holy servant of the Church, tireless and courageous in his zeal for souls. Manzoni is dexterous in his portrayal of Borromeo's sanctity, relating it with masculine matter-of-factness without ever stooping to the saccharine level of the hagiographic. The Nun of Monza is based upon a real-life noblewoman who, having been coerced into religious orders by her family, lives an embittered life, succumbing to the sin of fornication and its sordid ramifications. The fact that the pure and chaste Lucia is entrusted to the care of such a woman adds one more agonizing twist and turn to this most anguished of tales.

Apart from these leading players, a number of minor characters add their own inimitable *je ne sais quoi* to the story. The most memorable of these is Dr. Azzeccagarbugli, whose surname is rendered by the novel's translator as Dr. Quibbleweaver, which, aside from being quintessentially and delightfully Dickensian, is an apt appendage for a corrupt lawyer who weaves quibbles into hard cash for himself and his rich and equally corrupt clients.

One final aspect of Manzoni's novel needs to be mentioned. The whole work is imbued with good humour, itself an expression of the author's goodness, which alleviates the grimness of the novel's *gravitas* with the *levitas* of Christian hope. The narrative voice of the author, when it interjects itself into the story, is one which lightens and leavens the whole work with whimsy. It is the presence of the author's overarching and overriding Christian vision that trumps a note of triumph and even triumphalism into the darkest corners of the narrative. Irrespective of each ensuing catastrophic turn in events, one always senses in the gentle intrusion of the authorial voice that all will be well in the end. It does not matter how bad things are or how much worse they become. Even in the midst of the madness of the Machiavel or the massacre of the innocents, there is always the promise of final victory. It is the very essence of great Christian literature, which always sees the silver lining to every cloud, and the unseen sun that it signifies, knowing that the darkest of tragedies is always and ultimately subject to the divinest of comedies.

15

The Victorian Age in Literature

G. K. Chesterton devoted the first part of his book *The Victorian Age in Literature* to examining what he termed "The Victorian Compromise." He was alluding to the spirit of pragmatism, which was one of the chief characteristics of nineteenth-century England. Yet the essence of the Victorian Conundrum, of which Chesterton was a perspicacious observer, had as much to do with ineradicable Contradiction as with pragmatic Compromise. The age of Victoria (1837–1901) saw the rise of Empire and also the rise of anti-imperial nationalism; it saw the apparent triumph of industrialism and yet also the rise of an entrenched anti-industrialism; it saw the rise of capitalism and the birth of Marxism; it was the age of Darwinian science but also the age of Dickensian romance; it was the age of an emboldened atheism and yet the age of resurrected religion; it was the age of disillusioned agnosticism but also the age of returning faith. It was all these things, a cacophonous clash of contradictions masquerading as compromise.

JOHN HENRY NEWMAN

From a Catholic perspective, the most important figure of the Victorian Age is indubitably Blessed John Henry Newman, who had been received into the Church in 1845. It would, in fact, be no exaggeration to say that Newman's conversion was the very birth of the English Catholic Revival. Before Newman, the Catholic presence in England had withered to such a degree that only the remnant of the old recusant families still carried the Faith from one beleaguered and persecuted generation to the next. These courageous adherents to the "Old Faith" bore the Catholic Faith in their hearts and in their homes, but they were effectively excluded from bringing it into public life. After Newman's conversion, however, Catholics exercised a major intellectual influence in English culture, and, in Newman's wake, thousands of Englishmen followed his example, entering the Church in droves. This phenomenon crossed the Atlantic, heralding a similar revival in the United States.

If Newman's historical importance is beyond question, then so is the great legacy he has bequeathed to posterity. In theology, philosophy, education, and literature he has bestowed an abundance of riches on the Church and the world. In 1833 he published his first book, *The Arians of the Fourth Century*. Many of his finest poems, including "Lead, Kindly Light," were written around this time, and it was also in this year that the Oxford Movement, of which Newman would be the leading light, came into existence.

Newman's last great sermon as an Anglican was entitled "Development in Christian Doctrine," a sermon he preached in February 1843. This understanding of doctrinal development has had a profound influence ever since, and it helped to elucidate the teaching authority of the Church's Magisterium in the light of the ecclesiology surrounding the Church as the Mystical Body of Christ. His discourses on liberal education, delivered to Catholic audiences in Dublin in 1852, as he prepared to become rector of the new Irish Catholic University, would be published two years later as *The*

Idea of a University, a book that remains one of the finest and most eloquent works advocating the efficacy of an integrated liberal arts education. His greatest contribution to philosophy is his seminal work *The Grammar of Assent* (1870), the product of twenty years' labour, which highlighted the inadequacy of empiricism and the rational foundations for religious belief. His *Apologia pro Vita Sua* (1864) is arguably the greatest autobiographical spiritual aeneid ever written, with the obvious exception of St. Augustine's incomparable *Confessions*.

Years earlier, in 1848, only three years after his reception into the Church, Newman had foreshadowed his *Apologia* with his first novel, *Loss and Gain*, a fictionalised quasi-autobiographical account of a young man's quest for faith amid the scepticism and uncertainties of early-Victorian Oxford. He also addressed the issue of conversion in his historical novel, *Callista: A Sketch of the Third Century*, published in 1855.

As a prose stylist, the critic George Levine judged Newman as "perhaps the most artful and brilliant prose writer of the nineteenth century," a judgement seemingly echoed by James Joyce, via Stephen Dedalus, in *A Portrait of the Artist as a Young Man*. Newman was also one of the finest poets of the Victorian age, evident especially in "The Sign of the Cross," "The Golden Prison," and "The Pilgrim Queen," which rank alongside the best verse of his illustrious contemporaries. His most ambitious poem is *The Dream of Gerontius*, later the inspiration for an oratorio by Sir Edward Elgar, which presents the vision of a soul at the moment of death, and its conveyance by its guardian angel to the cleansing grace of Purgatory. "It reminds us at times of Milton," suggested the critic A. S. P. Woodhouse, "and it strikingly anticipates T. S. Eliot in its presentation of Christ as the surgeon who probes the wound in order to heal." Newman's *Dream* was also greatly admired by C. S. Lewis, who drew on what he called its "right view" of Purgatory as one of the inspirational sources for his own purgatorial excursion in *The Great Divorce*.

CHARLES DICKENS

It could be argued that, after Shakespeare, Dickens is the finest writer in the English language. His works have forged their way into the canon to such a degree that it is much more difficult to know which of his novels to leave off the recommended reading list than it is to choose which to include. Each of us has our favourites, and each invariably begs to differ with his neighbour's choice.

In terms of pure brute statistics, *A Tale of Two Cities* is his bestselling novel, with sales exceeding 200 million, but those who are justifiably sceptical of the claim that the bestselling is necessarily the best might point to a poll conducted by the Folio Society, a *de facto* private members club for bibliophiles, as a more objective way of judging the best of Dickens as opposed to the most popular. More than ten thousand members of the Society voted in 1998 for their favourite books from any age. *The Lord of the Rings* triumphed; *Pride and Prejudice* was runner-up; and *David Copperfield* was third. Why, one wonders, was this particular Dickens classic selected ahead of *Nicholas Nickleby*, *Oliver Twist*, *Great Expectations,* or *Bleak House*? Who can possibly know? It is a mystery as insoluble as that surrounding Edwin Drood in Dickens's last, unfinished work. In any case, and irrespective of these populist and elitist judgments, none of these Dickensian heavyweights wins the vote of the present author, whose favourite work by Dickens is the perennially popular tale of the conversion of Ebenezer Scrooge, as told in *A Christmas Carol*.

Originally published in 1843, *A Christmas Carol* is sandwiched chronologically between *Barnaby Rudge* and *Martin Chuzzlewit*, much weightier tomes. Yet Dickens's ghost story not only punches beyond its weight but outpunches its heavyweight rivals. Switching metaphors, the character of Ebenezer Scrooge, like a genie released or unleashed from a bottle, escapes from the pages of the book to charm the collective psyche of the culture. He is a literary colossus who, without the benefit of eponymous billing, has emerged from Dickens's imaginary menagerie as a cautionary icon of mean-spirited worldliness. Serving as a "mirror of scorn and pity towards Man," which Tolkien considered one of the chief characteristics of all good fairy-stories,[1] Scrooge has shone across the generations as a beacon of hope and redemption, as powerful parabolically as the Prodigal Son of which he is a type.

It is significant, as the story begins, that Dickens makes a comparison between the ghost of Jacob Marley and the ghost of Hamlet's father. In Shakespeare's play as in Dickens's story the ghosts serve to introduce not merely a supernatural dimension to the work but a supernatural perception of reality. The ghosts reveal what is hidden to mortal eyes. They see more. They serve as supernatural messengers who reveal crimes that would otherwise have remained hidden. Their intervention is necessary for reality to be seen and understood and for justice to be done. Thus, in connecting Jacob Marley's ghost to the ghost of Hamlet's father, Dickens is indicating the role and purpose of the ghosts that he will introduce to Scrooge and to us. They will show us not only Scrooge but ourselves in a manner that has the power to surprise us out of our own worldliness and to alert us to the spiritual realities that we are prone to forget.

Marley's ghost, like the ghost of Hamlet's father, is apparently a soul in Purgatory and not one of the damned. This is evident from its penitential and avowedly Christian spirit and its desire

---

1   Tolkien highlighted this characteristic of the function of fairy stories in his famous lecture and essay "On Fairy-Stories."

to save Scrooge from following in its folly-laden footsteps. When Scrooge seeks to console him with the reminder that he had always been "a good man of business," Marley's ghost wrings its hands in conscience-driven agitation. "Business!" he cries. "Mankind was my business. The common welfare was my business; charity, mercy, forbearance, and benevolence, were all my business. The dealings of my trade were but a drop of water in the comprehensive ocean of my business!"

If Marley's ghost is the spirit of a mortal man, suffering penitentially and purgatorially for its sins, the Ghosts of Christmases Past, Present, and Yet to Come are best described as angels. They are divine messengers (*angelos*, in Greek, means "messenger"). More specifically, they might be seen as Scrooge's own guardian angels, as can be seen from the first Ghost's description of himself as not being the Ghost of Long Past but of Scrooge's own past.

The final aspect of *A Christmas Carol* that warrants mention, especially in light of its poignant pertinence to our own meretricious times, is its celebration of life in general and the lives of large families in particular. The burgeoning family of Bob Cratchit, in spite of its poverty or dare we say because of it, is the very hearth and home from which the warmth of life and love glows through the pages of Dickens's story. At the very heart of that hearth and home is the blessed life of the disabled child, Tiny Tim, which shines forth in Tiny Tim's love for others and in the love that his family has for him. His very presence is the light of charity that serves catalytically to bring Scrooge to his senses. After his conversion, Scrooge no longer sees the poor and disabled as being surplus to the needs of the population who should be allowed to die, as in our own day they are routinely killed or culled in the womb, but as a blessing to be cherished and praised. For this love of life, even of the life of the disabled, *especially* of the life of the disabled, is at the heart of everyone who knows the true spirit of Christmas as exemplified in the helplessness of the Babe of Bethlehem. "And so, as Tiny Tim observed, God bless Us, Every One!"

GERARD MANLEY HOPKINS

In 1866, Blessed John Henry Newman received a young man by the name of Gerard Manley Hopkins into the Church who was destined not only to become a Jesuit priest but to become arguably the greatest and most influential poet of the Victorian Age. His *magnum opus,* "The Wreck of the Deutschland," is one of the greatest poems ever written and one of the most penetrating into the mystery of suffering. Unfortunately, space precludes any discussion of this deepest and most challenging of poems, not least because it would take a whole book to do it any sort of justice. We will, therefore, restrict our discussion of Hopkins to a brief appraisal of "God's Grandeur," a short and more accessible poem which encapsulates all that Hopkins represents in terms of his poetic vision.

The opening line of this marvellous poem—"The world is charged with the grandeur of God"—says all we need to know about the world in which we are living. Every time we see a tree, resplendent in countless shades of green and washed in sunlight, we see the presence of the goodness, truth, and beauty of God. Every time we see anything in God's Creation, shining forth its splendid self like shook foil, to borrow another image from Hopkins's poem, we are seeing the presence of the Creator himself.

Hopkins's greatest gift is the way that he shows us the grandeur of God in Creation, teaching us how we are meant to see, with eyes wide open with wonder. He shows us the difference between the wandering mind and the wondering soul. Whereas a mind may wander aimlessly like a cow grazing in a field, its head down, intent only on satisfying its animal appetites, it may also look up and see the glory that surrounds it. Whereas the animal only grazes, a slave of instinct and appetite, man is called not merely to graze but to gaze.

"We are all in the gutter," wrote Oscar Wilde, "but some of us are looking at the stars." When Hopkins looked up, he did not just see the stars, he saw the "moth-soft Milky Way" with its "belled fire" ringing forth God's glory, calling us to prayer and praise. And after the daily resurrection of the dawn, he did not just see the sky, he saw the "jay-blue heavens."

"Again, look overhead," he urges us. "Nay, but do but stand where you can lift your hands skywards. . . . The glass-blue days are those when every colour glows, Each shape and shadow shows."

It takes a soul blessed with humility to be able to see as Hopkins sees, with wonder-filled eyes that can contemplate the miracle that surrounds us, for, as Chesterton says, we do not live in the best of all *possible* worlds but the best of all *impossible* worlds. We are in the presence of a miracle, of which we are ourselves a miraculous part. "Give me miraculous eyes to see my eyes," writes Chesterton. "Those rolling mirrors made alive in me, terrible crystals more incredible, than all the things they see."[2]

And yet there are none so blind as those with pride-filled eyes, blinded by their own prejudice. Hopkins also laments such blindness and the stumbling, fumbling way that it desecrates the beauty and majesty of God's grandeur.

Generations have trod, have trod, have trod;
    And all is seared with trade; bleared, smeared with toil;
    And wears man's smudge and shares man's smell: the soil
Is bare now, nor can foot feel, being shod.

We can no longer see because we have blinded ourselves with the pride that shuts the eyes to wonder. We can no longer feel because we have covered and smothered ourselves

---

2   G. K. Chesterton, "The Sword of Surprise."

with artificial accretions. *Nor can foot feel, being shod. . . .* We have sold the real reality, which shines forth God's grandeur, for thirty pieces of tarnished silver, exchanging it for a tawdry virtually real substitute, distracting ourselves to death with the wasted time that prevents us taking the time to see the goodness, truth, and beauty that surrounds us.

It is only the great gift and blessing of humility that can liberate us from our self-absorbed selves, for, as Hopkins shows us, we can only kiss the sky if we learn how to kneel. This is an admonishment to astonishment! We need to learn, with humble hearts, to be astonished by the presence of beauty. For it is only in the presence of beauty that we will see the presence of the Beautiful Mind that brought such things into being. Mindful of such a Beautiful Mind, Hopkins ends "God's Grandeur" with these wonder-filled and contemplative lines:

> And for all this, nature is never spent;
> There lives the dearest freshness deep down things;
> And though the last lights off the black West went
> Oh, morning, at the brown brink eastward, springs—
> Because the Holy Ghost over the bent
> World broods with warm breast and with ah! bright wings.

FRANCIS THOMPSON

> *I fled Him, down the nights and down the days;*
> *I fled Him, down the arches of the years;*
> *I fled Him, down the labyrinthine ways*
> *Of my own mind . . .*

There was a time when the opening lines of Francis Thompson's poem "The Hound of Heaven" would have been widely known. Today, the poem and the poet are almost entirely forgotten, as is made manifest by the scandalous neglect of his gravesite in

Kensal Green cemetery. Such ignorance of fine art and such forgetfulness of a priceless heritage say more about the demise of England than they say about the neglected legacy that Thompson has bequeathed to a heedless nation. It is indeed ironic that the decaying gravesite serves as a living metaphor of England's decay. Like the picture of Dorian Gray in Oscar Wilde's novel, the ugliness of the neglect reflects the ugliness of England's neglectfulness, a mirror of her own decadence, decay, and impending death. And yet, in the forgetful fog of such amnesia, it is important that Catholics rediscover this wonderful poet.

Francis Thompson, having failed in his efforts to train for the priesthood and then for the medical profession, lived for a while in abject poverty in the squalor of post-Dickensian London. Homeless, penniless, addicted to laudanum, and sleeping on the streets, he befriended prostitutes at a time when the notorious Jack the Ripper was filling those same streets with terror. He spent some time recovering his health and overcoming his drug addiction at Storrington Priory in Sussex, a monastic community which was immortalized a few years later by Hilaire Belloc in his poem, "Courtesy":

> On Monks I did in Storrington fall,
> They took me straight into their Hall;
> I saw Three Pictures on a wall,
> And Courtesy was in them all.

The recipient of the same courtesy that would so impress Belloc, Thompson recovered remarkably well at Storrington, writing some of his finest verse during his period of convalescence with the monks, including his most famous poem, the earlier-quoted "Hound of Heaven."

Although most revered as a poet, Thompson was also the author of "Finis Coronat Opus," one of the finest short stories the present author has ever had the pleasure of reading. A cautionary tale in the Faustian mode, it tells of a poet who sells his soul to the devil and sacrifices his marriage on the altar of "art." It was a stinging sideswipe against the rising aesthetic movement with its mantra of "art for art's sake" and its desire to divorce beauty from morality. Here, as elsewhere and always, Thompson's art was always at the service of the good, the true, and the beautiful.

Francis Thompson died in 1907 at the tragically young age of forty-seven. He was eulogized memorably by G. K. Chesterton, who described him as "the greatest poetic energy since Robert Browning." "In Francis Thompson's poetry, as in the poetry of the universe, you can work infinitely out and out, but yet infinitely in and in. These two infinities are the mark of greatness; and he was a great poet."[3]

Returning to the vision of the neglected grave in Kensal Green cemetery, there seems no more appropriate tribute to Thompson's life and death (and resurrection) than the closing lines of Chesterton's famous poem "The Rolling English Road":

My friends, we will not go again or ape an ancient rage,
Or stretch the folly of our youth to be the shame of age,
But walk with clearer eyes and ears this path that wandereth,
And see undrugged in evening light the decent inn of death;
For there is good news yet to hear and fine things to be seen,
Before we go to Paradise by way of Kensal Green.

One suspects that Chesterton had Francis Thompson in mind as he wrote these lines. Thompson's youth was certainly full of folly and the reference to seeing things "undrugged" is surely an allusion to the laudanum addiction that Thompson, like Coleridge before him, had never managed to overcome.

The final words on this great but neglected poet do not belong to Chesterton but to the God whom Chesterton

---

3   G. K. Chesterton, *All Things Considered* (London: Methuen & Co. Ltd., 1926), 206.

and Thompson worshipped. At the end of "The Hound of Heaven," it is Christ himself who speaks to the Poet:

> Alack, thou knowest not
> How little worthy of any love thou art!
> Whom wilt thou find to love ignoble thee,
>   Save Me, save only Me?
> All which I took from thee I did but take,
>   Not for thy harms,
> But just that thou might'st seek it in My arms.
>   All which thy child's mistake
> Fancies as lost, I have stored for thee at home:
>   Rise, clasp My hand, and come!

OSCAR WILDE

Apart from the notable conversions of Newman and Hopkins, there were other significant literary converts during the Victorian period, not least of whom was Coventry Patmore, a fine poet who would exert a considerable influence on the young C. S. Lewis. At the end of the Victorian Age, several of the major poets of the *fin de siècle* were received into the Church, including Ernest Dowson, Lionel Johnson, and John Gray. Aubrey Beardsley, the artist of the *fin de siècle* who in his short life became so important and such an influence on his contemporaries that Max Beerbohm dubbed the 1890s "the Beardsley Period," was also received into the Church shortly before his death in 1898. Apart from Beardsley, the most important figure of the *fin de siècle* was the allegedly incorrigible Oscar Wilde who finally consummated his lifelong love affair with the Catholic Faith with his reception into the Church on his deathbed in 1900.

Wilde wrote several first-rate plays, on which his literary reputation principally rests, and a number of mostly second-rate poems. He is also lauded, quite rightly, for his short stories, mainly for children, of which "The Selfish Giant" and "The Canterville Ghost" warrant special mention. His only novel, *The Picture of Dorian Gray*, remains one of the most potent cautionary tales about the dangers and destructiveness of a life of debauchery. It is one of the darkest and, at the same time, and paradoxically, one of the most moral of novels, and one of the finest ever written. It is, therefore, ironic that Wilde is not remembered by most people for his literary *oeuvre* but for the scandal surrounding his private life. Having deserted his wife and two young sons in pursuit of the homosexual lifestyle, he was sent to prison in 1895. Demonized by his contemporaries for the moral iconoclasm of his sexual choices, he is now lionized by many as a "martyr" for the cause of (homo)sexual "liberation." The risibly inappropriate nature of the latter judgment is made manifest by Wilde's description of his own homosexuality as a "pathology," a statement that could land him in gaol in some European countries in our own "liberated" age for the heinous crime of "homophobia."[4]

Wilde would not have been happy with the manner in which his literary achievement has been partially eclipsed by the sordid and squalid details of his private life. "You knew what my Art was to me," he wrote to Lord Alfred Douglas, his "friend" and nemesis, "the great primal note by which I had revealed, first myself to myself, and then myself to the world; the real passion of my life; the love to which all other loves were as marsh-water to red wine." He died in disgraced exile, in Paris, fearing that future generations would see only the

---

4   For further reading on Wilde's views on homosexuality see Joseph Pearce, *The Unmasking of Oscar Wilde* (San Francisco: Ignatius Press, 2004).

marsh-water of his murky "loves," leaving the wine of his Art untasted. In his final hours he was received into the Catholic Church, being fortified and consoled by the Last Rites. It was the consummation of a lifelong and flirtatious love affair with Christ and his Church which stretched back to his days as an undergraduate in Dublin.

In the end Wilde was cured of his "pathology" by the healing hands of Christ as ministered by the priest who received him into the Church and who gave him the last rites. His sins forgiven, he was granted the saving embrace of Holy Mother Church on his deathbed, reconciled with the Bride of Christ *in extremis.*

We will not leave the final words to Wilde but to a kindred spirit, Ernest Dowson, a fellow Decadent, who, as mentioned, was also received into the Church. Writing with the beauty, eloquence, and gratitude of a truly repentant sinner, Dowson rejoiced at the saving power of the Last Rites of the Church in his poem "Extreme Unction":

> The feet, that lately ran so fast
>   To meet desire, are soothly sealed;
> The eyes, that were so often cast
>   On vanity, are touched and healed.

16

French Literature

Like all nations, France is an enigma. Admired by Hilaire Belloc for being the eldest daughter of the Church, she is also the harlot who sacrificed her own sons and daughters on the anti-Christian altars of secularist revolution. She has produced great sinners and even greater saints.

Legend traces the roots of Christianity in France to the time of the disciples, with none other than Lazarus, whom Christ had raised from the dead, being said to have been the first bishop of Marseilles. In the second century St. Irenaeus fought fearlessly to counter the threat of gnosticism before being martyred in Lyons in 202 AD. Almost three hundred years later, Clovis, the first of the kings of France, was baptized, renouncing his paganism and establishing France as a Christian nation. It was in France, at the Council of Clermont in 1095, that Pope Urban II preached the necessity of a just war in the Holy Land to free the holy shrines of Christendom from the grip of Islam, thereby triggering the First Crusade. Almost two hundred years later, a French King, Louis IX, would die while leading his army on the eighth crusade.

Perhaps the zenith of French power, at least in terms of her relationship with the Church, was in the fourteenth century, during which the seat of the papacy was removed from Rome to Avignon. Such power was also made manifest in the edifices of gothic architecture that sprung up across the country in the Middle Ages, such as Notre Dame de Paris and the cathedrals at Chartres and Reims.

The roll-call of French saints is so vast that one hardly knows where to start or finish. To name but an illustrious few, she can count among her canonized sons and daughters Bernard of Clairvaux, Joan of Arc, Martin of Tours, Thérèse of Lisieux, King Louis IX , Louis de Montfort, Vincent de Paul, Francis de Sales, and Jean-Marie Vianney. And yet she also gave birth to John Calvin, without whom the Protestant rupture would not have so tragically ripped Europe apart, and René Descartes, whose break with scholasticism signalled the rise of modern philosophy and the abandonment of philosophical realism, thereby condemning the modern world to the reductio *ad absurdum* of radical relativism. Pascal, a contemporary of Descartes and a fierce critic of Cartesian error, championed the Church during a period of rising secularism and theological error. His defence of Christianity continues to resonate across the centuries of modern French history as a consistent counterpoint of sanity amidst the oscillations between anti-Christian revolution and religious rapprochement.

The eighteenth century began with the rise of irrational "rationalism" and ended when the "noble savagery" of Rousseau metamorphosed into the ignoble savagery of Robespierre and the militaristic imperialism of Napoleon. Yet, if the eighteenth century can be characterized as a descent into the abyss of revolution and war, the nineteenth century produced some eloquent critics of the so-called and self-named Enlightenment, the most notable of whom were François-René de Chateaubriand, Louis Gabriel Ambroise de Bonald and Joseph de Maistre. The same century also saw the descent into decadence and the return to religion of such writers as Baudelaire, Verlaine, and

Huysmans, their respective conversions spawning a Catholic literary revival in France which paralleled the similar revival across the channel in England.

One reason for this renewal of faith in France during the nineteenth century, in spite of the gruesome efforts to snub it out at the end of the previous century by the terror-mongers of the Revolution, was the apparitions of the Blessed Virgin in Lourdes in 1858, the impact of which spread out from the Pyrenees until it reached the northern shores of the country, where, at the end of the century, St. Thérèse of Lisieux, described by St. Pius X as "the greatest saint of modern times," would charm the world with the humility of her "little way" to Heaven.

Moving into the twentieth century, France has brought forth the existentialist avant-garde, epitomized in the lives and works of Jean-Paul Sartre and Albert Camus, but she has also been the birthplace of neo-Thomism through the works of Jacques Maritain and Étienne Gilson. In addition, she has blessed the world with a veritable host of great Catholic writers in the past century, including, to name but a representative few, Georges Bernanos, Léon Bloy, Paul Claudel, Julien Green, François Mauriac, and Charles Péguy.

Perhaps the struggle between revolution and revelation in the turbulent and troubled heart of France can be epitomized in two of her daughters, Simone de Beauvoir and Simone Weil. Born in Paris within a little over a year of each other, in 1908 and 1909 respectively, Beauvoir was a radical feminist who refused to have children, sexually abused her female students, and boasted of having an abortion, whereas Weil turned towards the Catholic Faith following a mystical experience in Assisi. Such is the perennial war between revolution and revelation in the lives of these two daughters of France. Such is the war at the heart of France herself.

FRENCH WRITERS EVERY
CATHOLIC SHOULD KNOW

Having presented the contextual parameters within which any discussion of French culture and literature must reside, let us take a brief look at the history of French literature, pausing to focus on those writers of particular interest to Catholics.

The most important work of mediaeval French literature is the anonymously authored *Song of Roland*, a poem in the epic tradition celebrating Christian heroism in the wars with the infidel. Although inferior literarily to those works of mediaeval literature that we have already discussed, it is a work with which Catholics should be familiar.

The French Renaissance, spanning the years from the mid-fifteenth to the early seventeenth centuries, was something of a literary Golden Age. Key figures from this period include Charles of Orleans, François Villon, Clément Marot, Joachim du Bellay, Pierre de Ronsard, and François de Malherbe. According to Hilaire Belloc, who wrote a book on the poetry of the French Renaissance, Charles of Orleans "has a note quite new and one that after him never failed, but grew in volume and majesty," laying the foundations for the literary Renaissance which followed him. Belloc alluded to the lilt of his marching songs and to his "spontaneity and freshness." His verse is light but delightful, "simple, charming, slight," full of "spring and sureness." Belloc also noted that "[t]he poise of these light nothings make them a flight of birds."[1]

As for the poetry of Villon, best known for its lewdness and its flirtatious celebration of decadence, special mention should be made of his "Ballade of Our Lady," a work which is uncharacteristic in its expressive Catholic piety. According to Belloc, the lines of the poem, written by Villon as a gift to his

---

1   Hilaire Belloc, *Avril* (London: Duckworth, 1931), 23–24.

own mother, "pour from the well of a religion which has not failed in the place where Villon wrote, and they present that religion in a manner peculiar and national." Fulsome in his praise, Belloc declared unabashedly that "The Ballade of Our Lady" is "one of the masterpieces of the world."[2]

Moving on from the Renaissance to the so-called Enlightenment, we have already seen that France was afflicted by the rise of a particularly virulent form of secularist materialism which would lead to the tyranny of that nation's proto-communist revolution. One consequence was the reappraisal of Enlightenment ideas which followed in the wake of the Revolution's descent into the Reign of Terror. As in England, the literature of nineteenth-century France was characterized by various degrees of disillusionment with the cankerous and cantankerous ideals that had led to revolution. These conflicting and confused efforts to find a new ideological synthesis are apparent in the novels of Victor Hugo, whose most famous novel, *Les Misérables*, conflates and confuses the self-sacrificial love of the Christian with the ideological idealism of the Revolution. The novel is, to be sure, a literary masterpiece and, as such, warrants reading, but Catholic readers should be aware that Hugo, like many writers of his generation, was guilty of what George Orwell would call "double-think," which might be defined as the holding of two mutually incompatible viewpoints simultaneously.

One facet of nineteenth-century French literature that was destined to have a profound influence globally was what became known as the Decadence.

In one sense, the French Decadence could be seen as the decay of Romanticism, or as the logical and psychological decay of that Dark Romanticism which was manifested in English literature by Byron and Shelley. This Byronic

---

2   Ibid., 49–52.

Romanticism had crossed the English Channel and had found itself baptized in the Decadence of Baudelaire, Verlaine, and Huysmans, each of whom would plumb the depths of narcissistic despair, discovering therein the reality of Hell and recoiling in consequence and in horror into the arms of Mother Church. Baudelaire was received into the Church on his deathbed, Verlaine converted in prison, and Huysmans, having dabbled with diabolism, spent the final years of his life on the fringes of a monastery. The principal difference between the Dark Romanticism of Byron and Shelley and the Decadence of Baudelaire, Verlaine, and Huysmans is that the former delved into the darkness of their own egos with nothing but Nothing to illumine their musings whereas the latter delved deep into their own inner darkness with the light of theology. The former were lost in circumlocutions of self-centred circumnavigation, the latter discovered the Beast that dwelt in the bottomless pit of self-obsession and, beating their chests, knelt at last before the Christ that their own sins had crucified.

The writers of the French Decadence show us that the devouring of experience is dangerous and potentially deadly, prompting the asking of crucial questions: If the devouring of experience is the deflowering of the soul, who or what is being devoured and by whom? Did we devour the experience or were we devoured by it? Such questions were asked and answered by the Decadents whose insatiable appetite for the devouring of experience had led to frustration and desolation. They discovered that the soul is not merely the psyche, in the sense that "psyche" is understood by modern psychology. It is not to be understood by plumbing the depths of the ego but by acknowledging its source and its destiny in its Creator. It is indeed true that Baudelaire plumbed the depths of the ego-psyche in ways that few, if any, poets had plumbed before. He had gone deeper, or at least he had gone lower. In the end, he discovered, to his horror, that when you dig deep enough into the pride-centred self, you find the devil. And having made the discovery, he recoiled in disgust into the saving arms of Mother Church. In short, Baudelaire discovered, after all his searching, the truth about the soul that had already been discovered by Dante and by the Metaphysical Poets, Southwell and Crashaw. If Baudelaire had read Southwell he could have plumbed the depths of true psychology (*psyche* and *logos*) discoverable in Ignatian spirituality. If he had read Crashaw, then he could have discovered the depths of the soul in the profound mystical theology of St. Teresa of Avila and St. John of the Cross. And of course, if he had read Dante, then he would have discovered the psychological depths discernible in the thought and teaching of St. Thomas Aquinas. Instead, Baudelaire, by a circuitously sinful route, discovered these deepest truths for himself in the very mistakes that he had made. The consummation of his quest for himself was the giving of his sin-scarred self to Christ.

If Dark Romanticism had crossed the Channel in Byronic guise, metamorphosing into the symbolism of the French Decadence, it re-crossed the Channel under the patronage of Oscar Wilde, who was an aficionado of Baudelaire and Verlaine. Wilde had read Huysmans's recently published Decadent masterpiece, À *Rebours*, during his honeymoon in Paris, a novel which would greatly influence his own Decadent tour de force, *The Picture of Dorian Gray*. As with their French predecessors, and as we have seen, the doyens of the English Decadence also found their way to the Catholic Church, turning their back on debauchery and modernity in favour of traditional Christianity.

Should Catholics read the works of the French Decadence? One might hesitate to answer definitively one way or the other. It depends so much on the individual reader's own sense and sensitivity. And yet, regardless of whether Catholics should read these works, it is imperative that they know about them, which is why they warrant the time and space we have spent on them. The conversion of so many of the authors of these works teaches us the timely and timeless lesson that the literature of death and decay can sometimes prophesy the poetry of resurrection.

As we conclude our brief survey of French literature, moving into the twentieth century, it must be acknowledged that modern and postmodern literature in France is often associated with the nihilistic existentialism of Jean-Paul Sartre and Albert Camus. This dark and despairing literature is not, however, the whole story, nor is it the part of the story that should most interest Catholics. As with England, France experienced a dynamic Catholic literary revival in the twentieth century, the fruits of which deserve and demand our attention, albeit only in passing with only the briefest of glances.

Perhaps the best known of all the works of the French Catholic literary revival is *Diary of a Country Priest* by Georges Bernanos, a work which should be on the reading list of every Catholic, as should *The Woman Who Was Poor* by Léon Bloy. Although Bloy is best known as an essayist, this particular novel is a minor classic, even if not as overtly or obviously Catholic as is Bernanos's better-known work. Another significant figure in the French Catholic revival is Paul Claudel, a dramatist whose work exhibits his devout faith explicitly and unapologetically. Of all his plays, *The Satin Slipper* is the best known in the English-speaking world and is the most celebrated in France, being listed in *Le Monde*'s 100 Books of the Twentieth Century. Last but not least of those *eminenti* of the Catholic literary revival in France whom anglophone Catholics should know is François Mauriac, a winner of the Nobel Prize in literature, whose novels convey the presence of grace in the contortions of the human heart.

Should only one of his novels be recommended above the others it would have to be *Vipers' Tangle*.

In closing this chapter on French literature, and as a sort of postscript, we are going to add Franz Werfel's *The Song of Bernadette*. Technically it does not belong here, since it was written and first published in German, but it would clearly be a grave sin of omission to fail to mention this marvellous novel about the Marian apparitions at Lourdes. As space constraints preclude a separate chapter on German literature, we are permitting ourselves the poetic license of adding a work that is set in France, even if it was not originally written in French.

17

Russian Literature

For those who are old enough to remember the chill of the Cold War, it is all too easy to forget that Russia is part of Europe and, indeed, that she is an integral part of Western Civilisation. Ironically, the very fact that she succumbed to the seductive lies of communism is itself proof that she is part of Europe. The radical secularism which spawned communism sprang from the ideas of the Enlightenment, especially as expressed by French, German, English, and Scottish philosophers. The prototype of the Russian Revolution was the French Revolution which preceded it by more than a century. As for the founding fathers of the communist creed, Karl Marx and Friedrich Engels were both Germans who spent much of their lives in England. It could be argued, therefore, that Russia had fallen under the spell of Western European ideas in embracing the communism that would lead to the founding of the tyrannical Soviet Union.

Leaving philosophy and politics aside, there is no denying that culturally Russia is part of that collective inheritance which is called Christendom. According to tradition, the Russian Orthodox Church was founded by the apostle St. Andrew, which takes Russian Christianity back to the very dawn of Christianity itself. Even were one to treat such claims with scepticism and accept instead a more prosaic interpretation of history, the roots of Russian Orthodoxy still go back to the ninth century. The very concept of Holy Mother Russia demonstrates that for many Russians their love of their nation is inseparable from their nation's Christian identity.

A further demonstration of Russia's place of honour within Western Civilisation is evident in the impressive list of classical composers with whom she has blessed the world, including Borodin, Khachaturian, Mussorgsky, Prokofiev, Rachmaninov, Rimsky-Korsakov, Shostakovich, Stravinsky, and Tchaikovsky, to name but an illustrious few. As for Russian literature, the list is equally impressive, including, roughly in chronological order, Pushkin, Gogol, Tolstoy, Dostoyevsky, and Solzhenitsyn.

Many consider Alexander Pushkin to be the greatest of all Russian poets. Influenced deeply by the ideas of the French Enlightenment, especially as preached by Diderot and Voltaire, one would think that Pushkin's works would be inimical to Christianity. Such a conclusion, however, would be unjust. His most celebrated and influential work, *Eugene Onegin*, is a novel written in narrative verse, or, more specifically, in a series of narrative sonnets. It tells the story of a superficial dandy who spurns the love of an idealistic young lady. Years later, after the young lady has married someone else, he tries to persuade her to elope with him. Although she confesses that she still loves him, she refuses to desert her husband, indicating that she has matured beyond the romantic naiveté of her youth into the fullness of a love rooted in responsibility and the courage that it necessitates. As for the eponymous protagonist, he is left to regret that his earlier superficiality and refusal to embrace the responsibility that marriage demands has left him with nothing but regrets for how things might have been.

Also noteworthy is Pushkin's short verse drama, *Mozart and Salieri*, which was used as the libretto for Rimsky-Korsakov's opera of the same name and served as the source and inspiration for Peter Shaffer's play *Amadeus*, which would later be adapted into an Oscar-winning film.

It is difficult for those who cannot read Russian to appreciate the majesty of Pushkin's language or to understand why he is so revered by his own countrymen as their nation's greatest poet. It takes a truly fine translation to hint at the beauty of the original verse, one which is the work of one who is not only fluent in the language but is himself a great poet. It is for this reason that Maurice Baring's translations of Pushkin's verse are to be recommended, especially his rendering of the despondency of "Remembrance" and his graceful re-presentation of "The Prophet," the latter of which, perhaps Pushkin's most famous poem, is a mystically epiphanous vision of the poet's thirst for the presence of the divine in the desert of his exile which ends with the words of God to the poet-prophet, calling him to baptize the world with his words:

> Then in the desert I lay dead,
> And God called unto me and said:
> "Arise, and let My voice be heard,
> Charged with My Will go forth and span
> The land and sea, and let My Word
> Lay waste with fire the heart of man."

If most people would agree that Pushkin commands the accolade as the greatest Russian poet, it would be more difficult to gain a consensus as to who deserves the laurel as the greatest Russian novelist. Some would argue for Tolstoy, others for Dostoyevsky, and some perhaps for Solzhenitsyn.

For Maurice Baring it was Leo Tolstoy who was second only to Pushkin. "The prose of Tolstoy is simple and natural," Baring wrote, "without rhetoric or emphasis, and extraordinarily vivid."[1] And yet, for all this natural simplicity,

---

1 Baring, *Have You Anything to Declare?*, 218.

there remains much confusion over the apparent conflict between the straightforward moral vision of Tolstoy's greatest novels, *War and Peace* and *Anna Karenina*, and the ethical stance arising from his somewhat peculiar quasi-religious and pseudo-socialist philosophy. The conflict is resolved once we understand that his great novels were written, mercifully, before he became infected with the odd ideas which dominated his later life and lesser works. Chesterton encapsulated this abyss which separates the essentially orthodox Christian vision of Tolstoy's great novels from the facile fanaticism of his later philosophy when he contrasted "the great moral which lies at the heart of all his work . . . the folklore simplicity . . . the ingrained belief in a certain ancient kindliness sitting beside the very cradle of the race of man" with "the trumpeting and tearing nonsense of the didactic Tolstoy, screaming for an obscene purity, shouting for an inhuman peace, hacking up human life into small sins with a chopper, sneering at men, women, and children out of respect to humanity, combining in one chaos of contradictions an unmanly Puritan and an uncivilised prig." It was, Chesterton insisted, "difficult in every case to reconcile Tolstoy the great artist with Tolstoy the almost venomous reformer. It is difficult to believe that a man who draws in such noble outlines the dignity of the daily life of humanity regards as evil that divine act of procreation by which that dignity is renewed from age to age."[2] This dichotomy or schism separating the essential Christian simplicity of the novels from the woeful philosophy of the author is exemplified by the simple fact that Tolstoy, as an old man, thought very little of the two works on which his reputation as a novelist rested. In old age he judged *War and Peace* and *Anna Karenina* to be unworthy of him, believing that they failed to reflect the philosophy that he now espoused.

---

2   G. K. Chesterton, *Twelve Types* (London: Arthur L. Humphreys, 1902), 148–150.

It is for this reason that Christians can feel very comfortable reading these novels, safe in the knowledge that the author of these masterpieces has much more in common with his Christian reader who appreciates them than he has with his older self who deprecated them.

Nikolai Gogol, another important and influential Russian writer worthy of our attention, was a playwright, novelist and writer of short stories. His literary style has been described as realist and surrealist, and as romantic and cynical. And yet, regardless of all such difficulties in categorizing or pigeonholing him, his importance and pre-eminence are unquestionable. "We have all come out of Gogol's Overcoat," wrote Dostoyevsky, referring to the influence of one of Gogol's short stories, the protagonist of which, Akaky Akakievich, exemplifies Russian literature's preoccupation with "the little person in the large impersonal city," the alienated misfit who sits uncomfortably within the environs of modernity. Although he could be said to be the prototype for the later Freudian musings of Franz Kafka, it must be said that Gogol's grasp of psychology in his characterization of Akakievich is much more penetrating than Kafka's or Freud's. He shows how suffering and a sense of shame can be the agent for spiritual growth, in specifically Christian terms, but also how it can be twisted into a hateful and hate-filled demonic force, unleashed with satanic fury. With the wisdom of hindsight, we can see Gogol's vision of the dangers of allowing pride to overcome humility as being truly and horrifically prophetic. It was the force of pride, made manifest in the communist mobs, which would unleash the reign of terror upon the people of Russia seventy-five years later, a politicized pride which transfigured and disfigured suffering into a hate-ridden and arrogant demonic force. Seldom has the power of the poet-prophet been more evident than in Gogol's nightmare vision of a world in which Christianity is rejected and its antithesis embraced.

If the Christian moral vision is implicit in Tolstoy's two great novels and in Gogol's influential short story, it is evident more obviously in the novels of Fyodor Dostoyevsky. In *Crime and Punishment*, the "crime," on the literal or physical level, is the murder committed by the novel's protagonist, Raskolnikov; yet, on the moral or metaphysical level, Raskolnikov's crime is the sin of pride and the nihilism to which it leads. It is Raskolnikov's pride which enables him to rationalize the justification for the murder; it is his pride which is the metaphysical malady which precedes the physical malefaction. The Christian presence is most evident in the character of Sonia, a destitute girl forced into prostitution by the penurious condition of her family. Raskolnikov ridicules her "feeble-minded" belief in God, countering it with his own proto-Nietzschean philosophy of self-justification: "He who dares much is right ... and he who dares more than anyone is more right than anyone."

"You have turned away from God," Sonia responds, "and God has struck you down and handed you over to Satan." In the end, it is the simplicity of Sonia's Christian love and not the complexity of Raskolnikov's philosophizing which brings the resolution and reconciliation that Raskolnikov needs.

Dostoyevsky's deeper philosophical intentions in the writing of the novel are revealed in the names that he gives to two of the principal characters. Raskolnikov derives from the Russian word *raskolnik*, which means one who splits, or breaks away, or dissents, indicative of Raskolnikov's cleaving himself from the grace of God and from right reason in his beliefs and the actions which are their consequence. By contrast, the name of Raskolnikov's loyal friend, Razumikhin, derives from *razum*, which means reason or rationality, illustrating his role as one who shows the indissoluble union of faith and reason, thereby offering the remedy for Raskolnikov's fracturing of faith *from* reason.

Dostoyevsky's next novel, *The Idiot*, was an attempt to portray a genuinely and authentically good man, a "holy fool," and how such holy foolishness is perceived as nothing but idiocy by the fool's worldly-minded neighbours. We have seen in our discussion of *Don Quixote* how Cervantes's fictional knight had served as an inspiration to Dostoyevsky in his portrayal of Prince Myshkin, the "idiot," and it is clear that he was also inspired by Pushkin's chivalric ballad "The Poor Knight." In twentieth-century literature, G. K. Chesterton sets out to portray his own quixotic "idiot" in the character of Innocent Smith in the novel *Manalive*, and Myles Connolly does something very similar with the eponymous hero of his novella *Mr. Blue*. In all of these cases, the author endeavours to show us the deep wisdom inherent in true innocence, or what might be called the childlike qualities necessary for the attainment of the Kingdom of Heaven.

If Dostoyevsky presents us with a kind of Christ figure in the character of Prince Myshkin in *The Idiot*, he affronts us with the very antithesis in the diabolical character of Stavrogin in *Demons* (sometimes called *The Possessed* or *The Devils*). In a dark, violent, and grim satire on the nihilistic forces which were threatening revolution in Russia, Dostoyevsky presents to us, in Stavrogin, one who prophesies the ideas of Nietzsche and the ideology of the Bolshevik revolutionaries. "I neither know nor feel good and evil," Stavrogin says, "and that I have not only lost any sense of it, but believe that there is neither good nor evil…and that it is just a prejudice."[3] We are scarcely surprised to discover that such a person, animated by such a philosophy, should be capable of the most horrific crimes.

Although the three novels by Dostoyevsky mentioned thus far are all thoroughly recommended, as is his excellent novella *Notes from Underground*, his masterpiece is indubitably *The*

---

3   Quoted in Joseph Frank, *Dostoevsky: A Writer in His Time* (Princeton, NJ: Princeton University Press, 2009), 646.

Brothers Karamazov. In this marvellous work, we are given Father Zosima, one of the most compelling depictions of a saintly soul in all of literature, and, in the novel's hero, Alyosha, we are shown a saint in the making. In Alyosha's brother, Ivan, we are shown the spirit of modern disillusionment with religious faith, and especially an antagonistic disdain for organised or institutional Christianity. This is made manifest in the famous Grand Inquisitor episode in which Ivan shows the Catholic Church to be a betrayer of the person and the teachings of Christ. It has been claimed that this episode displays Dostoyevsky's anti-Catholicism, but we should be careful of making such a sweeping assertion. Although the Grand Inquisitor who denies Christ is a member of the Spanish Inquisition and is therefore a representative of the Catholic and not the Orthodox Church, we need to remember that Ivan's point in telling the story is that all institutional religion has betrayed the Gospel. We need to recall that Ivan's voice is the voice of anti-Christian scepticism, a counterpoint to Alyosha, the Orthodox novice monk who is the novel's hero, and whose voice is the closest to that of the author, as is made clear from the fact that the narrator identifies Alyosha as the hero of the novel in the opening chapter, and a fact made even more explicit by the fact that Dostoyevsky says the same thing in his preface. Alyosha is not convinced by his brother's line of reasoning in "The Grand Inquisitor" and it is safe to assume that Dostoyevsky does not sanction such reasoning either. Dostoyevsky was a staunch supporter of the Russian Orthodox Church, and, although he was not by any means sympathetic to Catholicism, he had pro-Catholics, such as Vladimir Solovyov, as close and trusted friends.

In Solzhenitsyn, we have not only one of the greatest writers of the past century but one of recent history's greatest heroes. There can be no better way to conclude our appreciation of great Russian literature than by honouring the life and work of such a man.

For those who do not know this twentieth-century giant, a few of the principal facts of his life should be given. He was born a century ago, in December 1918, a little over a year after the Bolshevik Revolution had unleashed its terror on his motherland. Suffering the brainwashing mechanism of Soviet education, he became an avowed atheist and a believer in the secular fundamentalism of the communist regime. Then, while serving in the Red Army during World War II, he made the fatal mistake of writing critical comments about Soviet leader Josef Stalin, in private letters to a friend. Since there was no such thing as private correspondence in the Soviet Union, his letters were read by the authorities, and he was subsequently sentenced to eight years of hard labour for expressing his private opinions.

Solzhenitsyn considered the experience of being arrested and then imprisoned as an unmitigated blessing because it allowed him to see through the lies of the Soviet system and to perceive the evil which he had been deluded by propaganda to believe was good. In Solzhenitsyn's eyes, the knowledge of truth outweighed any suffering that was necessary for its attainment. "Bless you prison," he wrote in *The Gulag Archipelago*, "bless you for being in my life. For there, lying upon the rotting prison straw, I came to realize that the object of life is not prosperity as we are made to believe, but the maturity of the human soul." This priceless lesson had also been learned by Dostoyevsky, who believed that his life had been positively transformed by his own sufferings as a political prisoner: "It was a good school. It strengthened my faith and awakened my love for those who bear all their suffering with patience."[4] In this, as in so much else, Dostoyevsky and Solzhenitsyn can be seen to be kindred spirits.

In March 1953, having served his sentence, Solzhenitsyn suffered the further torment of being diagnosed with what

---

4   Quoted in D. M. Thomas, *Solzhenitsyn: A Century in His Life* (London: Little, Brown and Company, 1998), 194.

was believed to be terminal cancer. Faced with such suffering and the imminent prospect of death, he made a final embrace of Christianity, becoming a convert to Russian Orthodoxy, a decision which marked the pivotal point in his life. If he had died, he would have become one of those unrecognized millions of heroes of whom later generations would know nothing, another forgotten victim of twentieth-century tyranny. As it was, he made a remarkable, some might say miraculous, recovery.

Thereafter he set about exposing the horrors of Soviet communism, documenting in book after book the ugly facts that the Soviets had sought to keep hidden from the world. His novella *One Day in the Life of Ivan Denisovich*, which is certainly the one work of Solzhenitsyn's that everyone should read, details the ordeal faced by political prisoners in the Soviet labour camps. In this, as in other works, such as *Cancer Ward* and *The First Circle*, we are shown how the acceptance of suffering, the taking up of one's cross, has redemptive power, purging the soul of its pride. In his three-volume history of the Soviet forced-labour prison system, *The Gulag Archipelago*, he did more than anyone to open the eyes of the world to the reality of communism. Having won the Nobel Prize for Literature in 1970, he survived an assassination attempt by the KGB in the following year and was expelled from the Soviet Union in 1974, being deported to West Germany. After spending twenty years in exile, first in Switzerland and then in the United States, he finally returned home to Russia in 1994, after the fall of communism, remaining an active voice and influencing politics in Russia until his death in August 2008.

18

Nineteenth-Century American Literature

It is difficult to know where to start or finish in any discussion of the connection between American literature and the Catholic Faith. The whole topic is fraught with complexity, as is the relationship between the American nation and the Catholic Faith, or American history and the Catholic Faith. There are few American writers who are unashamedly or unabashedly Catholic, whereas there are many who have an ambivalent relationship with the Faith, sympathizing in some ways and yet keeping a safe distance. Others are converts whose embrace of the Faith radically transformed their very approach to life and literature.

One such convert, who is often seen as the American equivalent of John Henry Newman insofar as his conversion was highly publicized and highly controversial, was Orestes Brownson. An almost exact contemporary of Newman, Brownson converted to the Faith in 1844, a year before Newman took the same life-changing and life-giving step. Thereafter, like Newman, he became a tireless defender of the Faith and an outspoken controversialist on many topics, especially through his published essays in *Brownson's Quarterly Review*.

Of the same generation as Brownson were three other major American writers, Nathaniel Hawthorne, Henry Wadsworth Longfellow, and Edgar Allan Poe, none of whom were converts to the Faith but each of whom were attracted to what might be called the Catholic aesthetic. Hawthorn's best-known work is his novel *The Scarlet Letter*, a work which counters the pharisaical tendency in Puritanism with a more authentically Christian understanding of charity. Hawthorne's late work *The Marble Faun* is often seen as indicative of his sympathetic attitude towards the Church, and his short story "Dr. Heidegger's Experiment" conveys a moral perspective entirely in harmony with Catholic teaching on Original Sin and concupiscence. An intriguing connection between Hawthorne and the Catholic Faith is the fact that his daughter, Rose, converted to the Faith, became a religious sister, and shouldered charitable work that has led to calls for her canonization. As Mother Mary Alphonsa, the name she took as Mother Superior of the order of Dominican Sisters she founded, she is now recognized by the Church as a Servant of God.

Longfellow, like Hawthorne, his lifelong friend, would never have countenanced conversion to Catholicism, and yet his work, like Hawthorne's, is often congruent with a Catholic aesthetic and sometimes displays implicit or even explicit Catholic sympathies. Nowhere is this more evident than in the marvellous narrative poem *Evangeline*, in which the devoutly Catholic heroine searches for her true love, the man to whom she had been betrothed until they were forcefully separated on the eve of their wedding. This wonderful poem also depicts the Catholic priest in heroic terms, accentuating his holiness and the wisdom which is its fruit. Last but not least is Longfellow's translation of Dante's *Divine Comedy*, indicative of his great admiration for Dante but also, surely, an indication that he had some understanding of the Thomism that informs Dante's work.

Edgar Allan Poe was fascinated by Catholicism throughout his life, as Michael Burduck has shown in his important essay "Usher's Forgotten Church." Although this does not often manifest itself in his work, it is evident implicitly in the confessional tone of his short story "The Cask of Amontillado" and is magnificently explicit in the Marian devotion of his poem "Hymn."[1]

One can scarcely discuss American literature in the nineteenth century without paying due attention to Harriet Beecher Stowe's *Uncle Tom's Cabin*, a novel which would literally change the course of history. Its sympathetic portrayal of black slaves and its depiction of the evils of slavery did much to raise awareness of the abolitionist cause and contributed in no small part to the circumstances that led to the Civil War. It is reported that Abraham Lincoln, upon meeting Mrs. Stowe at the White House in 1862, remarked that "you are the little woman who wrote the book that started this great war." A devout Christian, Stowe's work was intended to convert the hardened hearts of her readers, awakening their sympathy for the plight of the slaves. In showing the love of slave mothers for their children, and the suffering caused by the forced separation of parents from their families, she shows the dignity of the human person, regardless of race. She also exemplifies true sanctity in the character of Uncle Tom, to such a degree that he can be seen as a Christ figure. Taken as a whole, the novel is nothing less than a powerful call to national repentance.

If failure to pay due attention to *Uncle Tom's Cabin* would constitute a veritable sin of omission in any consideration of nineteenth-century American literature, it is equally true to say that failure to address the place and importance of *Moby Dick* would be similarly remiss. Herman Melville's epic may or may not be the product of a confused mind, but it has certainly produced a good deal of confusion in the minds of its critics.

---

1   Michael L. Burduck, *Usher's "Forgotten Church"?: Edgar Allan Poe and Nineteenth-Century American Catholicism* (Baltimore: The Edgar Allan Poe Society of Baltimore, 2000).

It is generally believed that its plot is mere scaffolding, erected to frame Melville's philosophical groping and grappling. The physical action is therefore subsumed within the metaphysical struggle.

Some have seen *Moby Dick* as a philosophical riposte to the naïve optimism of the transcendental idealism then in vogue, as expressed in the writing of Emerson and Thoreau, countering such optimism with a radical pessimism towards the unbridled individualism that the transcendentalists championed; others have seen it as a pouring forth of what Melville called the "power of blackness" inherent in the "Calvinistic sense of Innate Depravity and Original Sin." Still others have suggested that the novel derives its depth from the tension inherent in the clash of philosophies, especially in the war between rationalism and religion, or between empiricism and biblical literalism. And then there are those who see it as a critique of New England Christianity and the hypocrisy and concupiscence of human nature, marking it as a work similar in theme to *The Scarlet Letter*. Another critic posited the idea that Melville's novel was inspired by Alexis de Tocqueville's *Democracy in America*, which was popular in the United States at the time that Melville was writing *Moby Dick*, implying that Melville shared Tocqueville's concerns about the dangers of tyranny inherent in the shortcomings of democracy and wrote his novel as a protracted meditation on the subject. In this reading, Ahab is cast as the Machiavellian politician who manipulates and ensnares his crew so that he can wield dictatorial power. Other critics have seen the novel as the conveyer of a profoundly Christian worldview. Some have seen it as a momentous *memento mori*, reminding us of the Four Last Things: death, judgment, Heaven, and Hell; others have suggested that Ishmael serves as a Jonah figure who discovers the need for humility and that the novel, taken as a whole, points to the centrality of the Cross as the key to the meaning of life. Whatever its deeper meaning, there is little doubt that *Moby Dick* is worthy of the struggle which the reading of it demands. It is what might be called a *De Profundis* work, evocative of the penitential cry of the psalmist "from the depths" of his being.

Of the following generation of American writers, Mark Twain comes to mind as being preeminent, a writer whose *levitas* stands in stark contrast to Melville's *gravitas*. Like his literary predecessors, Twain would never have contemplated conversion, but his masterful study of St. Joan of Arc shows a heart and mind enamoured of the holy maid. Furthermore, Twain himself considered his fictional account of St. Joan's life to be the best book he ever wrote:

> I like Joan of Arc best of all my books; and it is the best; I know it perfectly well. And besides, it furnished me seven times the pleasure afforded me by any of the others; twelve years of preparation, and two years of writing. The others needed no preparation and got none.

Unsurprisingly, his sympathetic account of a Catholic martyr has met with hostility from those who despise the Church. George Bernard Shaw vilified Twain for writing so sympathetically of the saint, and his pious approach to the subject continues to antagonize and bemuse Twain's secularist admirers.

Twain's novel on Joan of Arc, published in 1896, brings the curtain down on our discussion of nineteenth-century American literature. It is now time to raise the curtain on a new century, crossing the Atlantic to survey the fruits of the Catholic literary revival in England.

19

Benson, Belloc, and Chesterton

In the early years of the twentieth century, three writers emerged as major figures in the Catholic literary revival. Robert Hugh Benson graced the early years of the century with many wonderful works of Catholic fiction, Hilaire Belloc's powerful and blustering voice called people to the sanity and sanctuary of Rome, and G. K. Chesterton's humour and humility, and his incisive wit and wisdom, ushered countless converts into the Church.

BENSON

The first of Robert Hugh Benson's novels, and the only one written while he was still an Anglican, was *The Light Invisible*, published in 1903, which he considered inferior to the novels he wrote as a Catholic. It was "rather significant" that it was popular among Anglicans whereas Catholics appreciated it to "a very much lesser degree." "Most Catholics, and myself among them," Benson said, "think that *Richard Raynal, Solitary* is very much better written and very much more religious."[1]

Richard Raynal, Solitary evokes with beguiling beauty the spiritual depth of English life prior to the rupture of the

---

1 Robert Hugh Benson, *Confessions of a Convert* (Sevenoaks: Fisher Press, 1991), 60–61.

Reformation. It is a mini-masterpiece in which Benson seamlessly wove the modern storyteller's art with the chivalrous charm of the Middle Ages. Resembling a modern equivalent of *The Little Flowers of Saint Francis*, this genial and ingenious mingling of the modern and the mediaeval produces a hero who combines courage and sanctity in equal measure. Finding himself at home in the early fifteenth century in Richard Raynal's England and in the presence of the colourful character of "Master Richard" himself, the reader relishes the time spent with this holy hermit on his God-given mission. This is Christian literature at its most beautiful, at once both edifying and efficacious. Its power is purgatorial. It purges. It cleanses. It makes whole. Ultimately it shows that the roots of romance are in Rome.

Perhaps the clearest evidence of Benson's genius is to be found in the ease with which he crossed literary genres. Aside from his historical romances, he was equally at home with novels with a contemporary setting, such as *The Necromancers*, a cautionary tale about the dangers of spiritualism, or with futuristic fantasies, such as *Lord of the World*. The latter deserves to stand beside Huxley's *Brave New World* and Orwell's *Nineteen Eighty-Four* as a classic of dystopian fiction. In fact, though Huxley's and Orwell's modern masterpieces may merit equal praise as works of literature, they are patently inferior as works of prophecy. The political dictatorships that gave Orwell's novel-nightmare an ominous potency have had their day. Today, his cautionary fable serves merely as a timely reminder of what has been and what may be again if the warnings of history are not heeded. Benson's novel-nightmare, on the other hand, is coming true before our very eyes.

The world depicted in *Lord of the World* is one where creeping secularism and godless humanism have triumphed over religion and traditional morality. It is a world where philosophical relativism has triumphed over objectivity and where, in the name of tolerance, religious doctrine is not tolerated. It is a world where euthanasia is practiced widely and religion hardly practiced at all. The lord of this nightmare world is a benign-looking politician intent on power in the name of "peace," and intent on the destruction of religion in the name of "truth." In such a world, only a small and defiant Church stands resolutely against the demonic "Lord of the World."

If Benson's literary output encompassed multifarious fictional themes—historical, contemporary, and futuristic—he also strayed into other areas with consummate ease. His poems, published posthumously, display a deep and dry spirituality, expressed formally in a firmly-rooted, if sometimes desiccate, faith. The same deep and dry spirituality is evident in *Spiritual Letters to One of His Converts*, also published posthumously, which offers a tantalizing insight into a profound intellect. A series of sermons, preached in Rome at Easter 1913 and later published as *The Paradoxes of Catholicism*, illustrates why Benson was so popular as a public preacher, attracting large audiences wherever he spoke. Particularly remarkable is Benson's masterly *Confessions of a Convert,* which stands beside John Henry Newman's *Apologia pro Vita Sua* and Ronald Knox's *A Spiritual Aeneid* as a true classic in the literature of conversion.

In Benson's novel *Come Rack! Come Rope!*, first published in 1912, the whole period of the English Reformation is brought to blood-curdling life. The reader, if he allows himself to be carried thither, will find himself transported to the late sixteenth century, the terror and tension of the times gripping him as tightly as it grips the leading characters, who witness courageously to their faith in a hostile and deadly environment. According to the Jesuit Philip Caraman, the novel "quickly became established as a Catholic classic" and remains "perhaps the best known" of Benson's novels.[2]

---

2   Philip Caraman, S.J., Foreword to Robert Hugh Benson, *Come Rack! Come Rope!* (Long Prairie, MN: Neumann Press, 1995), v.

The inspiration for the novel came from the account of the Fitzherbert family in Dom Bede Camm's *Forgotten Shrines*, published in 1911, and from Benson's own visit, in the same year, to the Fitzherbert house in Derbyshire, where he preached at the annual pilgrimage in honour of the Catholic priest-martyrs Blessed Nicholas Garlick and Blessed Robert Ludlam, who were executed in 1588. From the blood of these martyrs came the seed of Benson's story. The novel's title is taken from the famous promise of St. Edmund Campion that he would remain steadfast, "come rack, come rope." Campion was executed in 1581.

This novel, arguably Benson's finest, is also a great romance, a great love story. It is a story that shows the romance of Rome and the true greatness of a noble and self-sacrificial love between a man and a woman. The love between Robin and Marjorie, the two principal characters, is a love far greater than that between Romeo and Juliet. Their love for each other has none of the possessiveness of Shakespeare's "star-cross'd lovers" and everything of the purity and passion of his Cordelia. As a love story alone, *Come Rack! Come Rope!* deserves its place in the canon.

As for the novel's climax, one must agree with Hugh Ross Williamson that "it is impossible not to be moved by the last chapter."[3] For potency and poignancy, the novel's climactic moment compares in literary stature with the final, fateful moments of Lord Marchmain in Waugh's masterpiece, *Brideshead Revisited*. And if Benson's finale lacks the subtlety of Waugh's denouement it matches it for dramatic tension.

Why, one wonders, does Benson's mini-masterpiece, which warrants comparison with the works of Waugh, remain largely unknown? One suspects that it has a good deal to do with the sad and sorrowful, and sinful and cynical, times in which we live.

---

3   Hugh Ross Williamson, Introduction to Robert Hugh Benson, *Come Rack! Come Rope!* (London: Burns & Oates, 1959), 5.

In healthier times, for which we can hope and pray, it will be regarded as the minor classic that it is. We can also hope that its author, so long neglected, will once more be seen among the stars of the literary firmament, his own star once more in the ascendant.

HILAIRE BELLOC

Belloc is one of a rare breed that, today, might be considered an endangered species. He was a man of letters; a man who refused to be pigeonholed, who refused to be labelled, who refused to be restricted by any sphere of speciality. Mercifully, he lived in an age in which the mania for specialization had not yet triumphed, in which it was not yet necessary to kowtow before the "experts" on any given subject, which had not yet suffered the disintegration caused by the compartmentalization of the academic disciplines into self-imposed excommunication from each other, and in which philosophers still knew theology, and in which historians still knew philosophy. He lived in an intellectually wealthier and healthier age than our own.

He counted among his friends and enemies other men of letters who similarly refused to be pigeonholed. Amongst his contemporaries were George Bernard Shaw, H.G. Wells, and G. K. Chesterton, each of whom wrote on anything and everything from philosophy and theology to history and politics. They expressed their ideas in fiction and non-fiction, in poetry and prose, in full-length books, and in journalistic essays for the newspapers. To put the matter plainly, these men and others like them engaged the culture with the beauty of words and the stimulating power of ideas. They sought to change society by changing the culture of ideas which informed society's perception of itself. They were exciting men living in exciting times.

Hilaire Belloc was educated in the benevolent shadow of the aging Cardinal Newman at the Oratory School in Birmingham and then at Balliol College, Oxford. His first two books, *Verses and Sonnets* and *The Bad Child's Book of Beasts*, were published in 1896. The latter became an instant popular success prompting more of the same, including *More Beasts (for Worse Children)* in 1897 and *Cautionary Tales for Children* ten years later. Although these books for children (of all ages) are indubitably charming and enduringly funny, it is perhaps unfortunate that, for many, Belloc is remembered primarily for these relatively trivial sorties into children's literature rather than for the vast body of work, transcending several genres, which represents his true and lasting legacy.

As a poet, Belloc ranks alongside the finest of the twentieth century. For sheer rambunctiousness, there is the riotous invective of "Lines to a Don," Belloc's vituperative riposte to the don "who dared attack my Chesterton." For sheer indefatigable vigour, there is the romp and stomp of "The End of the Road"; for a doom-laden sense of the decay of England, there is the knell of "Ha'nacker Mill.'" For the mystical sense of the exile of life, there is the Yeatsian yearning betwixt faith and faerie that is hauntingly evoked in "Twelfth Night." For the dance of melancholy and mirth amid "the ruines of time" there is the hip, hop, clap of the scintillating "Tarantella."

Apart from his poetry, Belloc's most accomplished literary works are those hauntingly personal pilgrimages of the soul, *The Path to Rome*, *The Four Men*, and *The Cruise of the Nona*, in which the author waxes wistful and whimsical on the first things, the permanent things, the last things, and on the things (and the Thing) that give meaning to, and make sense of, anything and everything else.

These three "pilgrimages," taken together, might be dubbed "travel-farragoes," a distinct literary genre in which Belloc excelled. They are, at one and the same time, both travelogues and farragoes, linear narratives connected to a journey interspersed with seemingly random anecdotal musings on anything and everything. The overriding structure of each of these three works is, therefore, animated by the creative tension between the forward momentum maintained by the author's account of his pilgrimage and the inertial force of the tangential interruptions. As such, Belloc's travel farragoes are not for those who are in a hurry but for those who wish to saunter with the author in the leisurely pursuit of those things that are worth pursuing at leisure; and those things worth pursuing at leisure are, of course, the very things that are worth spending our whole lives getting to know better.

Belloc's place amongst the twentieth century's literary *eminenti* should not detract from his position as a scholar, particularly with regard to his reputation as a biographer and historian. His first biography, *Danton*, was published in 1899 and, thereafter, he would continue to write biographies of historical figures, specializing particularly, though by no means exclusively, in the figures of the English Reformation. These included studies of Cromwell, James the Second, Wolsey, Cranmer, Charles the First, and Milton. He also published panoramic studies of the whole period, such as *How the Reformation Happened* and *Characters of the Reformation*, as well as a four-volume *History of England*. His principal legacy as an historian falls into three areas. First is his seminal struggle with H.G. Wells over the "outline of history"; second is his groundbreaking refutation of the prejudiced "official" history of the Reformation; and finally is his telescopic and panoramic study of the "great heresies."

Having discussed the multifarious talents of this remarkable man it should perhaps be noted that Belloc is more than a man of letters, more than a poet, or a novelist, or an historian, or a political thinker. Ultimately he deserves to be remembered for the gargantuan nature of his personality. In his case, to an extraordinary degree, it is the man himself who breathes life and exhilaration into the work. When he is writing at his best, every page exudes the charisma of the author, spilling over with the excess of exuberance for which the man was famous amongst his contemporaries. From his legendary and fruitful friendship with G. K. Chesterton to his vituperative enmity towards H.G. Wells, Belloc always emerges as the sort of man who is often described as being larger than life. Strictly speaking, of course, no man is larger than life. In Belloc's case, however, perhaps more than almost any other literary figure of his generation, the man can be considered truly greater than his oeuvre. As such, his greatest works are those which reflect his personality to the greatest degree. Whether he is loved or loathed, and he is loved or loathed more than most, he cannot be easily ignored.

G. K. CHESTERTON

Born in 1874, G. K. Chesterton burst upon the literary scene as a journalist and controversialist at the beginning of the twentieth century and continued to pour forth works of effervescent wit and wisdom until his death in 1936. He was in every sense of the word a man of letters who indulged his magnificent and magnanimous gifts across every literary genre. As an essayist, he ranks among the finest stylists in the English language, peppering his prose with the lively spice of paradox. As a poet, he is remembered primarily for his poem *Lepanto*, about the Christian victory over the Muslim fleet in 1571, and also for his poetic epic, *The Ballad of the White Horse*, which recounts the struggles of the Christian king Alfred the Great, against the invading Vikings and their seemingly indomitable paganism. Other poems, such as "The Donkey," "The Secret People," and "The Rolling English Road," remain well-known and well-loved and are often anthologized. Others, such as "The Strange Music" and "The Crystal," are unjustly neglected. He was also a literary critic of the first order, writing studies of William Blake, Robert Browning, and Geoffrey Chaucer. His study of Charles Dickens was greatly admired by T. S. Eliot, and his panoramic survey, *The Victorian Age in Literature*, remains the best introduction to this golden age of English letters.

Chesterton's biographies of St. Francis of Assisi and St. Thomas Aquinas were enormously popular and have remained so, the latter being judged by the celebrated Thomist Étienne Gilson as one of the finest studies of Aquinas ever written. Chesterton's seminal apologetic works, *Orthodoxy* and *The Everlasting Man*, remain influential today and have been cited by many converts as having been instrumental on their journeys in faith.

No appraisal of Chesterton's legacy would be complete, however, without due consideration being given to the importance of his works of fiction. Best known for his invention of the priest detective Father Brown, Chesterton was also the author of several full-length novels, each of which can be classified as a theological thriller. His first novel, *The Napoleon of Notting Hill*, looks at the perennially important and perennially ignored principle of subsidiarity which had been taught by Pope Leo XIII in his encyclical *Rerum novarum* (1891) and championed by Chesterton and his friend Hilaire Belloc in their advocacy of what became known as distributism. Among the admirers of *The Napoleon of Notting Hill* was George Orwell, whose novel *Nineteen Eighty-Four* was inspired, at least in part, by Chesterton's book.

The Man Who Was Thursday is generally considered to be Chesterton's greatest fictional achievement. Subtitled "a nightmare," it has been compared with Franz Kafka's nightmarish *Metamorphosis*. Making such a comparison, C. S. Lewis, wrote that "while both give a powerful picture of the loneliness and bewilderment that each one of us encounters in his (apparently) single-handed struggle with the universe, Chesterton, attributing to the universe a more complicated disguise, and admitting the exhilaration as well as the terror of the struggle, has got in rather more; is more balanced: in that sense, more classical, more permanent."[4] In essence, *The Man Who Was Thursday* is Chesterton's exorcising of the spirit of nihilism which had led him to the brink of despair when he was a young man. Under the influence of the decadent aestheticism of Oscar Wilde, and seduced for a while by the radical pessimism of Schopenhauer, Chesterton had felt himself crushed by fundamental doubt in his youth. Emerging from this nihilistic nirvana and enlightened by its author's embrace of the philosophy of Christian realism, this great philosophical novel exposes the sophistry of irrational doubt with the clarity of faith and reason.

If *The Man Who Was Thursday* is Chesterton's deepest and most difficult novel, *The Ball and the Cross* is his brightest and most dazzling. It is a swashbuckling romp in which the two protagonists, an honest atheist and an honest Catholic, seek to fight a duel in defence of their principles. In endeavouring to do so, they find themselves at war with a world that puts convenience and pragmatism before self-sacrifice and principle. With its many twists and turns, the novel celebrates the value and virtue of the quest for truth amidst the worldliness of indifference.

Manalive contrasts the intrinsic wisdom of innocence with the wilful naïveté of cynicism. Its main character, the symbolically named Innocent Smith, is misunderstood because his innocence is inaccessible to those around him. He is so innocent that they think he must be guilty and so honest that they believe he must be lying. The novel is, therefore, a meditation on the nature and supernature of sanctity and serves

---

4   D. J. Conlon, ed., *G. K. Chesterton: A Half Century of Views* (Oxford: Oxford University Press, 1987), 71–72.

as an exposition of the reasons that saints are misunderstood by sinners and are indeed often martyred by them.

The Flying Inn is a rambunctious defence of traditional Christian freedom and conviviality in the face of the puritanism of Islam, on the one hand, and the secular asceticism of George Bernard Shaw and his ilk, on the other. Chesterton had criticized Shaw for his militant vegetarianism and teetotalism and for his belief that the state should impose its puritanically socialist will on the populace. The novel likens the temperance movement in the west, with its demands for the outlawing of alcoholic beverages, to the intolerance of Islam. As such, it serves as a prophecy of the experiment in Prohibition in the United States and also as a warning against the rise of socialist intolerance, epitomized perhaps by the rise of Hitler who, as a non-smoker, a vegetarian, and a teetotaller, represented the sort of secular asceticism that Chesterton lampoons in the novel, especially in his characterization of the novel's antagonist, Lord Ivywood. At its deepest, therefore, *The Flying Inn* is a celebration of Christian freedoms against the forces of non-Christian and anti-Christian intolerance.

In the broadest sense, Chesterton's enduring relevance is rooted in the manner in which he analysed the problems that plague modernity with a wit and wisdom that is charming and disarming, using the power of paradox and combining clarity with charity in a way that is difficult to resist. His greatest strength is the way in which he always insists on the indissoluble marriage of faith and reason. After reading Chesterton, we are inoculated from the poison of modernism and will never again confuse the *Heilige Geist* with the *zeitgeist*, the Holy Spirit with the Spirit of the Age. Furthermore, his omnivorous approach to truth-telling leads us to God whether we are reading one of his novels or poems, or one of his essays or biographies. Chesterton can start with a piece of chalk and lead us to God. He can be running after his hat and find that he is running after God. He can discuss Dickens and find God, or write history as though it is God's Story. He is a writer and an apologist for whom everything is charged with the grandeur of God. Always at the fore, however, is his *realism*, in the philosophical sense of the word. He is always at war with nominalism and relativism and always a defendant of the rational essence of reality. It is his absolute insistence, at all times, on the inextricable bond that exists between *fides et ratio* that makes him such a powerful force for good.

MAURICE BARING

It would surely be a sin of omission to fail to mention the work of Maurice Baring in the context of our discussion of Belloc and Chesterton. The three men were confreres whose friendship was immortalized in the group portrait entitled *The Conversation Piece* by Sir James Gunn. Although Baring is not as well-known as he once was, the best of his novels, which were bestsellers when they were first published in the period between the two world wars, are priceless gems in need of rediscovery by a new generation of readers. Of particular note are *C*, which is generally considered his masterpiece, *Cat's Cradle*, *Robert Peckham*, and *The Lonely Lady of Dulwich*. He was also a very fine poet as a perusal of his *Collected Poems* will verify.

It must be conceded that *C* will be hard-going for modern readers who will struggle with its slow pace and its profound engagement with great works of literature and music, the impact of which on the protagonist drives the plot. It is, however, well worth the necessary effort for those who are patient enough to persevere. The most accessible of Baring's novels is probably *Robert Peckham*, which, alongside Benson's *Come Rack! Come*

Rope!, is perhaps the finest historical novel ever written about the bloody period following the English Reformation.

The final words on this finest of writers, and the final judgment on the importance of his work, should be those of the French novelist François Mauriac. "What I most admire about Baring's work," Mauriac told the Catholic actor-writer Robert Speaight, "is the sense he gives you of the penetration of grace."[5] In this defining quality, Baring's novels share much in common with Mauriac's own novels and, as we shall see, with those of Evelyn Waugh as well.

---

5   Laura Lovat, *Maurice Baring: A Postscript* (London: Sheed & Ward, 1947), 4–5.

20

Siegfried Sassoon and T. S. Eliot

We now turn to two great poets of the twentieth century who recoiled in horror from modernity and its culture of death and found fulfilment in Catholic Christianity. The first, Siegfried Sassoon, wrote of the horrors of World War I; the second, T. S. Eliot, wrote of the nihilism of the wasteland that followed in the war's wake.

SIEGFRIED SASSOON

Like most of the great poets who have graced our civilisation, Siegfried Sassoon is not as well known today as he ought to be. He deserves our attention for the acerbic *gravitas* of the war poetry for which he is best known but also for the poetry and prose that he wrote after the war.

Since it is likely that many readers will be unfamiliar with this great and greatly neglected poet, it would be good to begin with a few facts about his life.

Born in Kent, in southeast England, in 1886, Sassoon's experience of the trenches of World War I embittered him. Although he fought with great courage, being awarded the Military Cross for gallantry in battle, he was angered by the conduct of the war and the wholesale slaughter that it unleashed. In a barrage of bitter invective, expressed in satirical verse which became very popular as the initial enthusiasm for the war began to wane, he vented his spleen against the politicians, journalists, and senior military officers, whom he believed responsible for enflaming and prolonging the carnage. Typical of this astringent verse is "Suicide in the Trenches":

> I knew a simple soldier boy
> Who grinned at life in empty joy,
> Slept soundly through the lonesome dark,
> And whistled early with the lark.
>
> In winter trenches, cowed and glum,
> With crumps and lice and lack of rum,
> He put a bullet through his brain.
> No one spoke of him again.
>
> You smug-faced crowds with kindling eye
> Who cheer when soldier lads march by,
> Sneak home and pray you'll never know
> The hell where youth and laughter go.

After the war, Sassoon's reputation as a writer of first-rate prose, as well as poetry, was sealed with the publication of the three volume quasi-autobiography *The Complete Memoirs of George Sherston*. In 1945, at the end of the second of the world wars which the century of "progress" had wrought, Sassoon's scepticism towards modernity and its vacuous promises was expressed in "Litany of the Lost" with razor-sharp eloquence:

> In breaking of belief in human good;
> In slavedom of mankind to the machine;
> In havoc of hideous tyranny withstood,
> And terror of atomic doom foreseen;
> *Deliver us from ourselves.*

Chained to the wheel of progress uncontrolled;
World masterers with a foolish frightened face;
Loud speakers, leaderless and sceptic-souled;
Aeroplane angels, crashed from glory and grace;
Deliver us from ourselves.

In blood and bone contentiousness of nations,
And commerce's competitive re-start,
Armed with our marvellous monkey innovations,
And unregenerate still in head and heart;
Deliver us from ourselves.

As the world stumbled from World War to Cold War, Sassoon befriended Father Ronald Knox, whose *God and the Atom* had expressed the same post-traumatic stress in the wake of the dropping of the atomic bombs on Hiroshima and Nagasaki as had Sassoon's "Litany of the Lost." Knox died in August 1957, and, a month later, Sassoon was received into the Catholic Church, a few weeks after his seventy-first birthday and a full forty years after Knox's own conversion.

Following his conversion, Sassoon, the war poet, became a poet of peace, a fact expressed in the title of the first volume of poetry he published as a Catholic. *The Path to Peace*, published in 1960, was essentially an autobiography in verse, ranging from the earliest sonnets of his youth to the religious poetry of his last years. Of the latter, his long meditative poem "Lenten Illuminations," written during his first Lent as a Catholic, is surely one of the finest Christian poems of the twentieth century, inviting comparisons with T. S. Eliot's "Ash Wednesday," which had also been written shortly after the poet's conversion. It is a monologue that the poet addresses to the ghost of his pre-convert self, musing on his life and how it had led him to his knees in a church.

Apart from the brilliance of the poetry in its own right, shining forth as a visible witness to the good, the true, and the beautiful, there is also a more prosaic and practical relevance to Sassoon's life and work. Having lived through two fratricidal world wars, fighting courageously in the first, and having become utterly disillusioned with the lifeless coldness of modern secular "progress," with which the world with devildom had gone dark, he had finally found the peace beyond all understanding which, as Eliot also discovered, was the only authentic escape from the wasteland of worldliness.

T. S. ELIOT

Thomas Stearns Eliot was almost an exact contemporary of Siegfried Sassoon. He was born two years after Sassoon, in 1888, and would die two years before him, in 1965. A native of St. Louis, Missouri, he came to Europe as a young man, studying in France before settling permanently in England. His vision and his work are, therefore, a hybrid of English, European, and American influences.

Although Eliot belongs on the long list of twentieth-century literary converts, he is nonetheless something of an odd man out. Unlike the others he never submitted to Rome, preferring to declare himself a "Catholic" within the Church of England, a so-called Anglo-Catholic. His reason appears to have been rooted in an Anglophilia bordering on Anglomania. As an American trying too hard to become an honorary Englishman, he imbibed the English prejudice against Rome and clung to the beleaguered belief that Anglicanism was somehow apostolic. As the neo-Thomist philosopher Jacques Maritain quipped, "Eliot exhausted his capacity for conversion when he became an Englishman." And yet, in spite of such folly, Eliot *is* a Catholic writer, much more so than that other great convert to Anglicanism, C. S. Lewis, and much more than some writers who actually belonged to the

Catholic Church, such as Graham Greene. Whereas Greene toyed with heterodoxy, playing with fire for the sheer hell of it, one would need to search hard for any infelicitous *faux pas* against orthodoxy in the works of Eliot. Greene, gangrened with doubt and self-loathing, lapsed into the folly of mortal sin, the fatal *felo-de-se*; Eliot, healed by faith and humility, rose to the fullness of grace, the fruitful *auto-da-fé*. Greene protested that he was not a Catholic writer but a writer who happened to be Catholic; Eliot ironically was very much a Catholic writer who happened not to be Catholic.

As for the age in which Eliot wrote, the 1920s and '30s, the age he condemned as a wasteland, it paralleled in many respects the wasteland that had provoked and inspired the Romantic reaction of Wordsworth and Coleridge more than a century earlier. Like his Romantic predecessors, Eliot was reacting against an atheistic anti-clericalism that had spawned a revolution. If Wordsworth and Coleridge were reacting against the debacle of the French Revolution, Eliot was recoiling from the debauchery of the Bolshevik Revolution. In "England, 1802" Wordsworth had described modern England as "a fen of stagnant waters," in which the wasteland of modernity takes the form of a swamp. Similarly, the allegorical dimension in Coleridge's "Rime of the Ancient Mariner" resonates uncannily with the fragmentary hints of conversion and resurrection which emerge in Eliot's "The Waste Land." In both these works the deepest truths are revealed tantalizingly through their being re-veiled tarantellically in a web of wyrd-woven intensity.

Let us look a little closer at the *avant garde* innovation of "The Waste Land," the fragmentary form of which reflected the fragmented brokenness of the modern world which it satirized. Like a modern-day inquisitor, Eliot questioned the value of modernity: "What are the roots that clutch, what branches grow out of this stony rubbish?" Nor was he afraid to answer his own question in scathingly blunt terms: "Son of man, you cannot say, or guess, for you know only a heap of broken images."

The poem presents a panoply of characters, as vain as they are vacuous, signifying the synonymous nature of vanity and vacuity. Empty heads and empty hearts leading empty lives. Unreal people in an unreal city. Virtual people in a virtual reality devoid of virtue. Such is the way that Eliot shows us the crowd of commuters flowing over London Bridge, their heads as full of brown fog as the suffocating smog through which they walk. "So many," says Eliot, echoing Dante, "I had not thought death had undone so many." Dead men walking.

The typist. A type we all know. A soul dehumanized by her mindless mechanical job and her mindless mechanical life. Her drying underwear, "perilously spread" and "touched by the sun's last rays," prophesy the loss of her virginity, which is sacrificed with passionless pathos as the "young man carbuncular" makes his move: "Exploring hands encounter no defence; his vanity requires no response, and makes a welcome of indifference." Having done with her, he bestows "one final patronizing kiss, and gropes his way, finding the stairs unlit." Mindless mechanical sex as a mindless mechanical distraction in mindless mechanical lives. "Well now that's done," she mutters to herself, "and I'm glad it's over." Will she say the same of her life when it, too, is touched by the sun's last rays? Is it as meaningless as her maidenhood?

"Nothing again nothing," writes Eliot. "Do you know nothing? Do you see nothing? Do you remember nothing?" In such lines, and in such a line of questioning, Eliot points a finger of scorn at those who refuse to see any meaning or purpose, or goodness or beauty, in human existence. "Are you alive, or not?" Eliot asks. "Is there nothing in your head?"

The poet, reacting in disgust against modernity's madness and seeking life-giving water in the arid desert of the wasteland, finds, at the moment of the poem's conclusion, the peace that passeth understanding and the faith that heals.

As "The Waste Land" illustrates, T. S. Eliot embodies the embattled soul of the poet in the modern world, writing verse in adversity so that the narcissistic soul of modern man might look up from the gutter in which he sees his distorted self-image to the heavens to which his soul is called and the Hell that awaits those who refuse the call:

> I will show you something different from either
> Your shadow at morning striding behind you
> Or your shadow at evening rising to meet you;
> I will show you fear in a handful of dust.

Those who see only their own self-centred shadows and not the goodness, truth, and beauty of reality are not truly alive. They are the walking dead in need of the resurrection and the life.

"The Waste Land" was written when Eliot was on the psychological trajectory that would lead to his final embrace of Christianity, as was "The Hollow Men," which echoed "The Waste Land" in its scornful pessimism about modernity. By contrast, the poetry that he wrote following his conversion is less exasperated and more full of that peace that passeth understanding that was prophesied at the conclusion of "The Waste Land." "Ash Wednesday," as its title would suggest, is full of the penitential spirit which is the fruit of a soul longing for unity with the Divine. His verse drama *Murder in the Cathedral* portrays the martyrdom of St. Thomas Beckett in a manner that is reminiscent of Greek tragedy and yet palpitates with contemporary relevance, dealing as it does with the encroachments of the secular state on the right to religious liberty.

Eliot's last great work, *Four Quartets*, is a set of four poems, woven together as a protracted meditation on the nature of time and eternity and man's perception and experience of it. It is a work of profound Christian mysticism, elevating Eliot into the presence of the great Christian mystics, such as Julian of Norwich, Teresa of Avila, and John of the Cross, all of whom haunt the poem as ghostly influences, and also placing him into the company of the great Metaphysical Poets.

It has been observed that Eliot's corpus, taken as a whole, can be seen to be analogous with Dante's *Divine Comedy*. His early poetry, such as "The Love Song of J. Alfred Prufrock," "The Waste Land," and "The Hollow Men," can be seen to belong to his "Inferno" period, in which he muses on modernity and its culture of death; the middle or "Purgatory" period, encompassing poems such as "Ash Wednesday," "Choruses from the Rock," and *Murder in the Cathedral*, depict a penitential penetration into the heart of man, signifying spiritual progress and growth; and the final "Paradise" period, represented by *Four Quartets*, conveys the soul's ascent into the presence of God and its desire for ultimate unity with the Divine. Although such an analogous appraisal and summary of Eliot's oeuvre is less than entirely satisfactory, it does indicate the poet's own spiritual progress and ascent, his journey towards God.

As for Eliot's place in the literary canon, it rests securely on his position as the most influential poet of the twentieth century. As for the finest poem of the twentieth century, it is hard to choose between "The Waste Land" and *Four Quartets*. Whether one prefers the former, a jeremiad of unsurpassed subtlety, or the latter, an ecstasy worthy of the mystic flights of St. John of the Cross, the conclusion remains the same and remains as unmistakable. T. S. Eliot is not merely a giant in his age but is a colossus who will cross the abyss of the ages. A great poet—and Eliot is surely one of the greatest—is not merely of "his age" but of all ages. *Atque in perpetuum, frater, ave!*

21

Evelyn Waugh and Graham Greene

*Conversion is like stepping across the chimney piece out
of a Looking Glass world, where everything is an absurd
caricature, into the real world God made; and then
begins the delicious process of exploring it limitlessly.*

Evelyn Waugh [1]

Evelyn Waugh's conversion to the Catholic Faith in 1930
sent shockwaves through the English literary establishment,
much as T. S. Eliot's conversion to the Church of England
had done two years earlier. What was so shocking was that
Waugh and Eliot were considered ultra-modern pioneers of
the literary avant-garde. How could such practitioners of all
things modern nail their colours to something as ancient and
as embedded in tradition as Christianity?

The answer lay in the fact that both men had sullied
themselves in the sordid reality of modern culture and had
turned away in disgust, seeking something with the *gravitas*
and goodness that modernity lacked. In "The Waste Land"
and "The Hollow Men," as we have seen, Eliot had exposed
contemporary culture as a desert inhabited by a lifeless
people devoid of any roots and from any connection with

---

1   Written in a letter to Edward Sackville-West; quoted in Michael de-la-Noy, *Eddy: The Life of
Edward Sackville-West* (London: The Bodley Head, 1988), 237–38.

the permanent things, sinking in a quagmire of narcissistic selfishness. Waugh, in his early novels, was doing much the same as Eliot. In *Vile Bodies* and *A Handful of Dust*, the title of the latter being plucked from a line from Eliot's "Waste Land," Waugh holds up a scornful mirror to his faithless and fatuous peers, exposing the ugly reality behind the fashionable façade.

In these early novels, awash with satirical wit and sardonic wisdom, Waugh was honing his skills, serving his apprenticeship in the storyteller's art, so that he could reach the maturity necessary to write *Brideshead Revisited*, his greatest work and arguably the finest novel of the twentieth century. Its finely delineated characters, realistically portrayed and representing multifarious aspects of contemporary English culture, are as memorable as those of Shakespeare or Dickens, alive with a supernatural intensity.

Although some Waugh scholars and aficionados might dissent from the view that *Brideshead Revisited* is his *magnum opus*, arguing that his late work the *Sword of Honour* trilogy best merits such an accolade, the present author would contend that *Sword of Honour* is a flawed and flabby work, too loose in construction and containing a host of largely superfluous characters. It would, no doubt, have benefited from the prudent application of an editor's scalpel, though one suspects that no editor would have been brave or foolhardy enough to suggest to the incorrigible and cantankerous Waugh that such edits were necessary. *Brideshead*, on the other hand, is a lean and essentially flawless work, with every word a necessary part of the whole and every character serving a providential or pivotal purpose in the story's grand design.

One cannot really discuss *Brideshead*, even one who strongly prefers literature to film, without reference to the superb film adaptation of the book produced for British television in 1981 (not to be confused with the recent and horribly crass Hollywood version). Starring Jeremy Irons as

Charles Ryder, and Anthony Andrews and Diana Quick as Sebastian and Julia Flyte, this eleven-hour extravaganza must rate as one of the most faithful adaptations of a great work of literature ever made, a fitting tribute to Waugh and his wonderful work. As if the three superb starring actors were not sufficient enough, the supporting cast includes such greats as Sir Laurence Olivier, Sir John Gielgud, and Claire Bloom, all shot on location amidst the splendour and grandeur of Castle Howard in Yorkshire.

Published in 1945, *Brideshead Revisited* traces the interaction between Charles Ryder, its ostensibly agnostic narrator, and a family of aristocratic Catholics. In the preface to the second edition, Waugh wrote that its theme was "the operation of divine grace on a group of diverse but closely connected characters." This authorial and therefore authoritative exposition of the theme is key, in the literal sense that it unlocks the deepest levels of meaning in the work. If the key theme is the operation of divine grace, it means that there is a hidden hand at work, a supernatural presence operating on the characters. It is as though the novel's chief protagonist is not any of the visible characters but is God himself, whose omnipotent and omniscient presence guides the narrative. From a Christian perspective, this is nothing less than realism, in the sense that it reflects reality. It is, however, very difficult for a novelist to suggest this presence without descending to the level of didacticism and preachiness, two traits that are usually destructive to the power of the Muse. It is, therefore, a mark of Waugh's brilliance that he succeeds with a theme that he himself described as "perhaps presumptuously large."

Although the author's epigraphic note (*I am not I: thou art not he or she: they are not they*) signifies the author's desire to distance himself from any of the characters, it is evident that there is much of Waugh's own pre-conversion self in the characterization of Charles Ryder, the agnostic narrator through whom we see the story unfold. And yet, with a stroke of subtle brilliance, Waugh subverts the agnosticism of the narrative voice through its being spoken by the older Ryder, recalling the events of his life from a mature middle-age, at which point, as we discover in the Epilogue, he has himself embraced the Faith. Thus, the narrator expresses the religious doubts of his youth from the perspective of one who now doubts those doubts. In this sense, it is hard to see Ryder without seeing a shadow of Waugh, musing upon his own loss of faith as a youth and his years as a hedonistic agnostic at Oxford. So, for instance, Ryder's account of the disastrous effects of theological modernism on his own faith as a schoolboy reflects those of Waugh's real-life experience at Lancing College. Similarly, Ryder's account of undergraduate decadence and debauchery reflects Waugh's own riotous hedonism at Oxford.

The menagerie of characters that breathes life into the novel is drawn with Dickensian dexterity, and, on occasion, with Dickensian grotesqueness, suggestive of caricature, as is the case with the effete mannerisms of Anthony Blanche, the sordid creepiness of Mr. Samgrass, and the sadistic humour of Charles's father, the last of whom was played to hilarious perfection by Sir John Gielgud in the British television adaptation. As for the Catholic aristocratic family with whom Ryder interacts, they are some of the most memorable characters in modern fiction. Lord Marchmain, who deserts his wife and family and takes up with a concubine in Venice, is "conscious of a Byronic aura, which he considered to be in bad taste and was at pains to suppress"; Lady Marchmain, the deserted wife and mother, is pious in her faith but unable to win the affection of her children; Lord Brideshead, the eldest of the children and heir to the estate, is Jesuit-educated, deeply pious but socially inept; Sebastian, Eton-educated and therefore ill-equipped to grasp the rational underpinnings of faith, is self-consciously self-centred and lacking the desire or ability to grow up and grasp the responsibilities of adulthood; Julia, the older of the two daughters, is as self-centred as her brother, though less self-consciously, and shares his resentment of the way in which faith is an obstacle to self-gratification; and, last but indubitably not least, Cordelia, the youngest of the family, who is pious and precocious in equal measure, reminding us of her famous Shakespearean namesake.

The dynamic of the plot flows in two directions. In the first half of the novel, Sebastian and Julia stray further and further from their mother's reach and further from the Faith with which they associate her. Sebastian descends into alcoholism and social dereliction, living a life of increased squalor in North Africa, whereas Julia makes a reckless and ultimately disastrous marriage to a cynical and ambitious politician and later begins an adulterous relationship with Ryder. After Julia had "shut her mind against her religion," we are told of the suffering that her children's apostasy is causing Lady Marchmain.

It is after Lady Marchmain's death that the tide begins to turn or, to employ the metaphor that Waugh borrows from G. K. Chesterton, it is after her death that there is the "twitch upon the thread" which begins to tug the prodigals back, a metaphor for the power of grace.

From a worldly perspective, it is easy to find in Lady Marchmain a convenient scapegoat whose relentless adherence to the Faith has alienated her husband and children (or two of them at least) from herself and her religion. This is indeed the way that the novel is often read and taught in our meretricious age, which explains why the director of the recent and lamentably bad Hollywood adaptation of the novel proclaimed that, in his version (or spin), God was the enemy.

If, however, we take Waugh at his word and expect to find the operation of divine grace at work in the story, we need to seek the supernatural dimension. If we see with these theologically-attuned eyes we realize that Lady Marchmain's influence on her husband and children does not cease upon her death. Apart from the power that the memory of her invokes, there is the very real power of her prayers, both before and after her death. Her ghost continues to haunt her family, in the benign sense that she intercedes for them. Furthermore, it seems that her intercessory prayers are answered in dramatic fashion as Lord Marchmain, Julia, and Sebastian return to the fold.

And yet in each case, the conversion of heart does not come without a great deal of suffering. "No one is ever holy without suffering," says Cordelia, and it is no surprise that the other powerful metaphor for grace that Waugh employs as the novel reaches its climax is that of an avalanche that destroys everything in its path. Ryder's life is left in ruins, swept away in the avalanche of grace that had brought Julia and her father back to the Faith. And yet, like every good Christian story, there is life after death, or, perhaps we should say, there is a resurrection.

GRAHAM GREENE

Greene's conversion to Catholicism in 1926 was influenced, in the first instance, by the fact that the woman whom he would later marry was herself a convert. It would, however, be a grave error to explain, or explain away, Greene's Catholic identity as little more than an effort to please the woman he loved. Other Catholic influences were also at work, such as his evident admiration for the works of Eliot and Chesterton. Greene's early novels, such as *Stamboul Train* and *Brighton Rock*, were set in Eliotic wastelands, inhabited by Eliot's hollow men, in which we nonetheless detect, as with Eliot's poems, the hinted, haunting presence of an (almost) invisible Christ. His second novel, *The Name of Action*, published in 1930, employed several lines from Eliot's "The Hollow Men" as its epigraph.

Greene's admiration for Chesterton emerged in his review of Maisie Ward's biography of Chesterton, in which he described Chesterton's *Orthodoxy*, *The Thing*, and *The Everlasting Man* as "among the great books of the age," and in which he also praised several of Chesterton's other books, including *The Ballad of the White Horse* and the novels *The Man Who Was Thursday*, and *The Napoleon of Notting Hill*. It is also significant that Greene would always consider Newman's *Apologia pro Vita Sua* as one of his favourite books.

If, therefore, Greene's faith can be seen to be genuine, it does not alter the fact that his practice of the Faith, and his expression of it in his works, was, at best, enigmatic, and, at worst, downright disreputable and heretical. And yet, paradoxically, Greene's troubled faith, and his marital infidelity, provided the inherent tension in the labyrinthine morality plays that are his novels.

Greene deserted his family shortly after the end of World War II, leaving his wife for another woman. Vivien Greene remembered vividly the day that her husband left: "It was very difficult with the children...We went upstairs into the drawing room and then he left. And I thought, well, I'll probably never see him again and looked out of the window that was facing the street, and he looked back for a minute, didn't wave, but looked back." This dramatic moment clearly haunted Greene as much as it haunted his wife because it emerges, ghost-like, in *The Quiet American* when the character of Fowler turns random memories over in his mind: "a fox . . . seen by the light of an enemy flare the body of a bayoneted Malay . . . my wife's face at a window when I came home to say good-bye for the last time."

Greene's contorted conscience twisted itself agonizingly through the plot of *The Heart of the Matter*, the novel he wrote shortly after his desertion of his family, in which the convoluted moral convulsions of Scobie left many critics squirming.

Whereas some writers, including Evelyn Waugh, Edward Sackville-West, and Raymond Mortimer, had suggested that Scobie was a sinful saint, others had seen only the sinner: "Scobie commits adultery, sacrilege, murder (indirectly), and suicide in quick succession," one correspondent wrote.

At the other end of the critical spectrum, the Jesuit C. C. Martindale described *The Heart of the Matter* as "a magnificent book," adding that its effect on one "hard-headed man to whom this book was given" had been to serve as "the last necessary stimulus" to his becoming a Catholic.[2] Another correspondent wished it to be "put on record . . . that one great sinner was so moved by Mr Greene's last book that he has completely changed his way of life and returned to the practice of the Faith."[3]

Greene's own response to the critical reaction indicated that these repentant sinners, rather than the novel's detractors, had the deepest affinity with his own understanding of the novel: "I did not regard Scobie as a saint," he wrote to Waugh, "and his offering his damnation up was intended to show how muddled a mind of good will could become when once 'off the rails.'"[4] Ironically these words would become prophetically autobiographical. The longer Greene remained "off the rails" the more muddled he became in his approach to his faith.

Another of Greene's novels, *The Quiet American*, serves as a meditation on the relationship between New World naiveté and Old World cynicism. The former is present in the transparent (and dangerous) shallowness of Alden Pyle, the latter in the world-weary depths of Thomas Fowler. Pyle is certain that "Democracy," "Freedom," and "America" are not only inseparable but that they are synonymous. It is almost as though they form an indivisible Trinity, as holy as the

---

2   Norman Sherry, *The Life of Graham Greene, Volume Two* (London: Viking, 1994), 298–99.

3   Ibid., 299.

4   Ibid.

Trinity of the Christians and as worthy of praise. This quasi-religious zeal turns every war for "Freedom" and "Democracy" into a jihad, with Pyle emerging as a fanatic for the cause of "America" in much the same way that Muslim terrorists emerge as fanatics for "Islam." It must be said, however, that Pyle is much more likeable than any Islamic fanatic and is even disarmingly charming in his simple, unquestioning faith in the Motherland.

But what of Thomas Fowler, the pathetically apathetic wastrel whose jaded presence dominates the novel? He is almost the antithesis of Pyle, the anti-Pyle. Whereas Pyle is puritanical and abstemious, Fowler is an opium-addicted decadent. Whereas Pyle is an idealist, albeit an idealist enslaved by an ideology, Fowler is cynically indifferent to all ideals. Whereas Pyle is decorously prim and proper in his dealings with women, and particularly in his chivalrous dealings with Phuong, the woman at the centre of his and Fowler's desires, Fowler is unremittingly self-serving in his carnal relations, deserting his wife and children and seeing in Phuong little more than a comfortable and convenient ménage, indulging her as an addictive habit which, like his opium habit, allows him to escape temporarily from his responsibility to reality. Whereas Pyle is motivated by an illusory Heaven on earth, a heaven of "democracy" and "freedom" (ironically, like that of his communist enemies), Fowler shuns Heaven and Purgatory and desires only the adulterous Hell of Paolo and Francesca in Dante's *Divine Comedy* (referring to an unwanted promotion that would force him to return to England, Fowler muses that "Dante never thought up that turn of the screw for his condemned lovers. Paolo was never promoted to Purgatory"). Pyle is willing to be a martyr for his false Heaven; Fowler tells Heaven (and Purgatory) to go to Hell. Who then is worse: the puritanically idealistic Pyle, or the morally iconoclastic Fowler? What is worse: messianic Americanism or the jaded, ethno-masochistic death wish of decadent Europe? New World naiveté or Old World cynicism? Should we choose one or the other, selecting the better of two evils; or are we at liberty, with Mercutio in Shakespeare's *Romeo and Juliet*, to call down a plague on both their houses?

And what of Graham Greene himself? Is it fair to associate him too closely with his fictional anti-hero, Thomas Fowler? It is true that, like Fowler, he deserted his wife and children; and it is true that, like Fowler, he settled into a number of adulterous ménages in the years after he left his wife. It is also true that, as with Fowler, his Christian (Catholic) wife would not contemplate a divorce (though Fowler's fictional wife eventually relented). Yet these similarities, though certainly not superficial, serve only to mask the very real differences that exist between the life and beliefs of the author and those of his fictional creation. Unlike the doggedly godless Fowler, Greene was, and remained (for the most part), a believing Catholic, a fact that separates him not only from Fowler but from the dogmatically godless type that he represents.

By the time that Greene wrote his play *The Potting Shed*, in 1957, even old friends and allies, such as Evelyn Waugh, were losing patience with his heterodox dabblings. The play was "great nonsense theologically," Waugh complained, "and will puzzle people needlessly."[5] Three years later, after Greene had written to Waugh of how his latest novel, *A Burnt Out Case*, was intended "to give expression to various states or moods of belief or unbelief" and that the characterization of the doctor had represented "a settled and easy atheism,"[6] Waugh had replied impatiently that many would see the novel "as a recantation of faith."[7]

---

5   Mark Amory, ed., *The Letters of Evelyn Waugh* (London: Phoenix, 1988), 502.

6   Ibid., 557.

7   Ibid., 559–60.

We can scarcely leave our discussion of Graham Greene without affording due consideration to his best known and most popular novel.

As with all literary criticism, an objective reading of the work requires an ability to see it through the eyes of the author, so far as this is possible. In seeing *The Power and the Glory* through the eyes of Graham Greene we perceive the whisky priest's almost demented impiety and anti-piety as a reflection of Greene himself. It is, for instance, significant that Greene chose the following words of Sir Thomas Browne, the seventeenth-century English author, as an epigraph to his first novel, *The Man Within*: "There's another man within me that's angry with me." It is as though Greene is himself the angry man within his characterization of the whisky priest, so much so that we can almost see the priest as being possessed by the angry and angst-ridden ghost of the author himself. Throughout the duration of the work, this authorial spirit whispers blasphemous thoughts into the protagonist's head, tempting him in the desert of his soul. Thus we see in *The Power and the Glory*, as in all of Greene's work, a genuine groping for religious truth grappling with the darkest recesses of the self-absorbed ego, the latter of which is often expressed with self-obsessive Baudelairean abandon. The consequence of such a struggle is the transposing of this darker side onto all of Greene's protagonists, so that even their goodness is warped. Greene saw human nature as "not black and white" but "black and grey," [8] thereby implicitly denying the purity of the divine image in man, and he referred to his need to write as "a neurosis … an irresistible urge to pinch the abscess which grows periodically in order to squeeze out all the pus." [9] Such a neurotic Muse can hardly fail to convey something of

---

8 Marie-François Allain, *The Other Man: Conversations with Graham Greene* (London: The Bodley Head, 1983), 134.
9 Ibid., 149.

its own pathology in the very fabric of the work it creates. It is, therefore, necessary to read the work with an eye to the authorial pathology within it.

Why is it that Greene was so seemingly allergic to the presence of purity and sanctity in his work that he would not admit even a modicum of childlike innocence amid the gloom of human degradation? Returning to our initial assertion that Greene obsessively transposed a darker side onto all of his characters, so that even their goodness was warped, we lament his apparent unwillingness or inability to allow even the children their innocence. Nobody is childlike in Greene's novels, not even the children themselves. Can anyone truly come to Christ in such dismal dystopias?

Although Greene, in his darker Mr. Hyde persona, is alarmingly and disarmingly convincing as the devil's advocate, he can also mock the devil's disciples, such as the Marxist lieutenant, the whisky priest's nemesis, by hinting that his belief in a godless cosmos is itself singularly "mystical." The atheist makes a leap of faith in Nothing as much as the theist makes a leap of faith in Something. It takes faith to believe in God, but it also takes faith not to believe in him. And thus Greene shows us one of the great jokes at the very heart of the human condition. Faith is essential, unavoidable. Even atheists cannot avoid acting on faith. Such is the provocative irony that drips from Greene's pen.

In his last years, Greene showed signs of returning to some semblance of orthodoxy, though it would be an exaggeration to describe his faith as "settled and easy." "I've betrayed a great number of things and people in the course of my life," he stated in 1979, "which probably explains this uncomfortable feeling I have about myself, this sense of having been cruel, unjust. It still torments me often enough before I go to sleep."[10] It is

---

10   Ibid., 20.

in this tormented light that we must view Graham Greene's relationship with his faith, his life, and his work. He never felt comfortable with the Catholic Faith but then he never felt comfortable with anything else either. Like St. Thomas the Apostle, whom Greene chose as his confirmation saint, he was a doubter. He doubted others, he doubted himself, and he doubted God. And yet the profundity of his novels never resides in the doubt itself but in the ultimate doubt about the doubt. It was this doubt about doubt that kept him clinging desperately to the Catholic Faith, so much so that his biographer, Norman Sherry, insisted that "he remained a strong Catholic until his death."[11]

---

11 Greene's biographer, Norman Sherry, in a letter to Joseph Pearce, September 26, 1996.

22

The Nordic Muse: Sigrid Undset

No appraisal of Catholic literature would be complete without paying due attention to Sigrid Undset, a Norwegian novelist and convert to the Faith, who would be awarded the Nobel Prize for Literature in 1928, four years after her reception into the Church. Her two most celebrated works are *Kristin Lavransdatter* and *The Master of Hestviken*, two historical epics set in mediaeval Norway, the first of which was published in three parts between 1920 and 1922 and the latter in four parts between 1925 and 1927.

Although *Kristin Lavransdatter*, unlike *The Master of Hestviken*, was written prior to Undset's conversion, the seeds of conversion are evident in the tone and tenor of the novel's plot, which follows the trials and tribulations of the eponymous heroine from her childhood to her death. The young Kristin betrays her family, and especially her wise and holy father, in her succumbing to wilful passion and its woeful and complex consequences. The reader winces as the young and headstrong girl makes mistake after mistake, failing to follow with faith and reason the path of wisdom and virtue. She learns from her mistakes, sometimes painfully slowly, by learning to live with their consequences, loving even as she is often deprived of the love she desires. It is as a wife and mother, embracing the struggle and suffering of married life, that she comes of age, seasoned by the experience of a life lived for others.

The novel is rooted in Norwegian history, of which Undset had a thorough knowledge, and in the spirit of the Norse sagas, which infuse its very spirit. The action is pedestrian in the best sense of the word, proceeding at the slow and steady pace of the seasons of the year and at the speed with which a person can travel either on foot or on horseback. Such pacing allows the reader to enter fully into the time in which the story is set by entering into the time taken by the characters themselves. This slows us down so that we can see with eyes unblurred by the pace and frenzy of modern life, inviting an unhurried contemplative approach to the events of the story as they transpire. This aspect of Undset's novel might remind some readers of the perambulations of the Fellowship of the Ring in Tolkien's classic, which is imbued with the same preindustrial pacing as *Kristin Lavransdatter* and shares the same heroic spirit of the Norse sagas, the love of which both authors shared and which influenced them as both inspiration and aspiration.

Although the pacing and historical and cultural backdrop might suggest analogies with Middle-earth, the development of character and the connection between actions and their consequences might invite parallels with the novels of Jane Austen or perhaps with *The Betrothed* by Manzoni. Certainly, Undset's characters suffer the consequences of their actions and come to wisdom through living with such consequences as do the characters in Austen's novels.

Undset's other great historical saga, *The Master of Hestviken*, is also set in mediaeval Norway and follows the sorrowful fortunes of Olav Audunssøn. As with Kristin Lavransdatter, the key characters gain consolation amid the maelstrom of life's misfortunes in their Catholic Faith and are fortified by the wise counsel of saintly bishops and priests.

Sigrid Undset's later works were mostly set in contemporary Norway but echoed the historical sagas in their portrayal of characters who learn from their mistakes, growing in sanity and sanctity thereby. The best known of these later novels is probably *Ida Elizabeth*, which shares with the earlier historical novels the author's profound understanding of the meaning of life and the manner in which her characters grapple with reality as a quest for that deeper meaning. Readers of *Kristin Lavransdatter* will note the recurrence of a familiar plot device as Ida Elizabeth learns to cope with an unfaithful and weak-willed husband and as she learns the meaning of life and love through her experience of being a mother in hard and distressful circumstances. And yet such motifs do not detract from the power of the story, nor from Undset's power as a storyteller. We suffer with the eponymous heroine as she hungers for true happiness, finding solace in the raising of her two boys but feeling unfulfilled in the sense that she lacks the fullness of life. It is only at the novel's close, and in a surprising way, that she finds the fullness of the love that had always eluded her.

Another of Undset's novels, even less known and even more neglected than *Ida Elizabeth*, is *The Wild Orchid*. Also set in contemporary Norway, the novel tells the story of Paul Selmer and his slow and faltering journey towards the Catholic Church. An unabashed "novel of conversion" that Undset had begun as early as 1919, five years before her own reception into the Church, but would not finish until ten years later, *The Wild Orchid* charts the protagonist's journey from scepticism to faith amid a backdrop of failed relationships. At the novel's culmination, Paul has still not taken the decisive step to submit himself to Holy Mother Church but appears on the brink of doing so. His final crossing of the threshold is told in the sequel, *The Burning Bush*, which leads him deeper into the mystery of life through the embrace of death, the ultimate paradox of the Christian life.

We cannot leave our discussion of Sigrid Undset without mentioning her heroic response to the rise of Nazism in the 1930s. In 1935 she published an essay entitled "Progress, Race, Religion," attacking the racist philosophy of the Nazis. In retaliation, all of her books were removed from German libraries and the Norwegian Nazi newspaper *Fronten* denounced her. In April 1940, the Nazis invaded Norway, forcing Undset to flee her home in Lillehammer. Six days later, her son was killed while fighting for the Norwegian army in a vain attempt to repel the German invasion. Forced to leave Norway as a political exile, she would spend the war years in the United States, returning to Lillehammer in August 1945. Her final work was an ambitious biography of St. Catherine of Siena, a saint who had always been a source of inspiration and an edifying model whom Undset had sought to emulate in her own life of deepening faith.

Sigrid Undset's legacy as a novelist is rooted in the realism of the scholastic philosophy of which she was a diligent student. Her novels expose the shallowness of relativism and exhibit the deepest metaphysical understanding of the bedrock morality on which all human life and society is founded. She sees the real world in which people face the bitter consequences of selfish choices and in which suffering is unavoidable, yet potentially redemptive. She sees this and shows it to her readers with a crystalline clarity enriched with Christian charity. At its deepest, her fiction shows us that the acceptance and embrace of suffering is not merely the beginning of wisdom, which it is, but also, and paradoxically, that it is the path to peace and lasting joy.

23

Twentieth-Century American Literature

Perhaps the two most important American writers of the early twentieth century, at least from a Catholic perspective, are T. S. Eliot, whom we have already discussed, and Willa Cather, who is best known for her novels about life on the American frontier, especially *O Pioneers!* and *My Antonia*, both of which are eminently worth reading. As with Mark Twain, nobody would suggest that Willa Cather would ever have contemplated conversion. Yet, as with Twain's *Joan of Arc*, she wrote one of the most Catholic of novels. *Death Comes for the Archbishop*, an historical novel based on the real-life adventures of a pioneering priest in the Old West who would become the first Archbishop of Santa Fe, New Mexico, warrants a place of honour in any self-respecting Catholic's library. Seldom has a non-Catholic author depicted the Catholic Faith so sympathetically and well as does Cather in this novel about a priest's slow and faltering growth in holiness.

Moving on to more recent writers, we come to Ernest Hemingway, a troubled convert to the Faith whose works are "Christ-haunted," if somewhat spiritually confused, and Flannery O'Connor, who coined the phrase "Christ-haunted" to describe the American South of which she wrote. Another writer on the literary roll of honour, who cannot be omitted, is Walker Percy, although here we can only offer a nod of deferential reverence in his direction.

With respect to Hemingway, we will defer to the judgment of the great scholar of his work, H. R. Stoneback, who stated that "the notion of pilgrimage" was the "ever-recurring center of Hemingway's work," serving as a "road map to the sacred landscapes of his fiction":

> What matters for students of Hemingway's writing . . . is that his fiction . . . is rooted in his religious sensibility, and the work is most deeply accessible through an understanding of his Catholic vision. Prose, Hemingway famously said, is architecture, not interior decoration. The spirituality, or if the reader prefers, the faith, the religion, the Catholicism of Hemingway's prose is architecture not mere interior decoration. And the foundational mode of that architecture is pilgrimage.[1]

Without wishing to disagree with Stoneback's appraisal of the Catholic identity of Hemingway's fiction, it must be said that it is often present in confused and confusing ways, reflecting the author's own troubled relationship with the Faith. In this respect, his work parallels that of Graham Greene. Both authors treat matters of faith with provocative ambivalence, undermining doctrine with the tension of moral ambiguity. As such, those reading their novels should not expect to find moral or theological coherence.

In contrast to the spiritual ambivalence in Hemingway, the work of Walker Percy is always infused, albeit subliminally, with an orthodox Catholic perspective of life which is simultaneously darkened with hints of the philosophy of Kierkegaard and lightened with whimsical satirical humour. He paints worlds in which the chill of rationalism and the cold-hearted callousness of scientism create a deep sense of alienation in the psyches of his characters, rendering their

---

1   H. R. Stoneback, "Hemingway's Sacred Landscapes," *St. Austin Review*, Vol. 19, no. 6 (January/February 2019).

existence almost surreal, devoid of meaning and divorced from reality. In such vacuity, the scream in the vacuum becomes a *cri de coeur*, an impassioned desire for the Real Presence of the Divine because its real absence is unbearable.

For the remainder of our discussion of twentieth-century American literature, we will turn to that giantess, Flannery O'Connor, taking a look at two of her short stories and one of her novels.

One of the most memorable characters to emerge from the gargoylesque pen of Flannery O'Connor is the Misfit in "A Good Man Is Hard to Find." He is savagely psychopathic and yet, at the same time, savagely sane. "I call myself The Misfit," he said, "because I can't make what all I done wrong fit what all I gone through in punishment." In perceiving himself as a hapless victim of injustice, he appears to be a kindred spirit with that other "madman," King Lear, who declared himself "a man more sinn'd against than sinning."

The problem with which the Misfit struggles, in his case unsuccessfully, is the conundrum at the heart of life itself. Why do we suffer, and do we deserve such suffering? This was the conundrum at the very crux of Chesterton's novel *The Man Who Was Thursday* which explores the mind's quest for meaning in the face of seemingly meaningless suffering. At the novel's end, we discover that it is the suffering of God himself that makes sense of all suffering, and it is through the suffering of Christ that Christians find meaning and purpose in their own suffering. The paradox is not that suffering is meaningless, as is claimed by the satanic accuser in Chesterton's novel or by the manically rational Misfit in "A Good Man Is Hard to Find," but that, on the contrary, it uncovers the very secret at the heart of life itself. Far from being senseless, it actually makes sense of ourselves and our place in the cosmos. It is not needless but necessary.

All of this was known and embraced by Flannery O'Connor, whose *acceptance* of her lifelong struggle with the debilitating effects of lupus is manifested throughout her work. Her experience of suffering, and the strengthening of faith and awakening of love that it heralded, could even be said to have been incarnated in her work, the pain serving as her Muse.

In "A Good Man Is Hard to Find" the real absence of this acceptance, as revealed by the Misfit's complaints about the suffering that he had experienced, leads to a desire to inflict suffering on others. The anger that is the bitter fruit of the Misfit's non-acceptance is literally deadly, reaping and wreaking havoc.

Solzhenitsyn lamented that the hedonistic modern world considered the acceptance of suffering as "masochism," yet here, in O'Connor's story, we see that the absence of such acceptance leads to sadism, and sadism of the most psychotic kind. The Misfit's refusal to follow the two great commandments of Christ, that we love the Lord our God and that we love our neighbour, leads to anger and the inevitable killing of both God and neighbour. A failure to love God leads to his Crucifixion; a failure to love our neighbour leads to the hatred of our neighbour, who becomes our enemy (and a subconscious hatred of ourselves also, as can be seen beneath the surface of the Misfit's words). God is Love; if we will not have God, we will not have love; and the absence of love is hatred, even if, in its slothful form, it makes a show of cynical indifference.

O'Connor presents us with another misfit in "Good Country People," a misfit who makes a dark art of cynical indifference. The ironically named Joy Hopewell even goes so far as to change her name to the deliberately ugly Hulga as a means of denying and defying the "joy" which was given to her at birth. In denying her Christian name she is denying Christianity itself, choosing the ugly alternative of nihilism instead. Hulga had declared war on "joy" as a bitter reaction to her losing a leg in a hunting accident as a child. Her whole philosophy of life is built on the bitterness of *unaccepted* suffering. Like the other Misfit, she feels that life has treated her badly and she hates life because of it, and, as for God, if he exists, he is the one responsible for her hateful life. The sin of pride, the source of her bitterness, is made evident by the fact that she has effectively declared herself the god of her own cosmos, a fact revealed by O'Connor through the words of defiance that Hulga directs to her mother: "If you want me, here I am—LIKE I AM." This is evidently a thinly veiled reference to the name that God gives to himself, when asked his name by Moses in the book of Exodus: *I Am Who Am*. This could be translated as Hulga utters it: "I am—LIKE I AM." Hulga has not only changed her name, she has changed her religion. She now worships herself alone. She has declared herself god of herself. This, of course, is the *de facto* position of all relativists. In refusing to accept the existence of absolutes, including truth itself, they make themselves the sole arbiters of reality.

Deceived by her pride into believing that she is not deceived by anything, Hulga tells Pointer, the Bible salesman, that "I don't have illusions. I'm one of those people who see *through* to nothing." The delicious irony is that she is being deceived by Pointer even as she is speaking. As he steals her wooden leg, she vents her venomous spleen against him and the religion she believes he represents:

> "You're a Christian!" she hissed. "You're a fine Christian! You're just like them all—say one thing and do another."

Again, she is deceived by her own credulous incredulity, which is made clear when Pointer responds indignantly that he does not believe "in that crap." His last words to her before disappearing with her leg represent the final comical *coup de grâce*: "And I'll tell you another thing, Hulga, you ain't so smart. I been believing in nothing ever since I was born!"

As with all of O'Connor's fiction the key to understanding the work is to be found on the level of allegory. In "Good Country People," the wooden leg is both the crutch and the crux of the story. It is the crutch upon which the whole story rests and the crux, that is, the cross, to which it points. The wooden leg is the cross that Joy/Hulga has been called to carry, that she is called to *accept* as Christ accepted his own Cross. In her refusal to accept her cross she sows the seeds of her own downfall. In refusing to accept her suffering with joy, it becomes the source of her bitterness, the root of her sin. Perhaps Hell is full of forsaken crosses. Perhaps it is from these that the damned hang eternally.

Flannery O'Connor knew that her readers would only begin to see the beauty of a life with Christ by seeing the ugliness of a world without him. She shows us the value of the light by showing us the darkness, reminding us that we do not value the good things in our lives, even our wooden legs, until we lose them. This is the truth to which the aptly named Pointer points.

The brilliance of O'Connor's use of the grotesque is that her stories bring the essential metaphysics to the surface. She presents us with gargoyles, such as the resentful Misfit and the joyless Hulga, in order to show us the face of the devil. Her grotesque conceits unmask the devil, to borrow the title of Regis Martin's excellent study of O'Connor, by removing the mask of the mundane that obscures the struggle of good and evil at the heart of reality. It is as if she picks up the stone with which we have hardened our hearts in order to reveal the nest of cockroaches, or serpents, lurking beneath. "My subject in fiction is the action of grace in territory held largely by the devil," she tells us, echoing the words of Dostoyevsky in *The Brothers Karamazov*: "The awful thing is that beauty is mysterious as well as terrible. God and the devil are fighting there, and the battlefield is the heart of man." This is the battlefield of which O'Connor writes, and it is the most realistic battlefield of all because it is the one on which we are all fighting, whether we like it or not, or know it or not.

Let us now turn our attention to Flannery O'Connor's second and final novel, *The Violent Bear It Away*. In page after relentless page in this dark work we are wrenched from our comfort zones, finding ourselves assaulted by the brute ugliness of a place in which the love of God has seemingly been exorcised. The sheer violence of it all is almost too much to bear, and yet we are borne away by it, wincing and squirming and yet unable to break the spell that O'Connor has cast on us, almost addictively desiring to know where the rollercoaster ride of misery is going to take us. However painful, we need to see it through to the bitter end.

For those who do not know the novel, and without wishing to spoil it for those who have not yet put themselves through the agonies of reading it, it centres upon a teenaged protagonist, Francis Tarwater, who has been brutalized theologically by his manically fideistic great-uncle, the latter of whom believes that his young protégé is called to be a prophet. The boy's upbringing, in which faith is emphatically divorced from reason, leaves him utterly unprepared to face reality. After his great-uncle's death, the boy goes to stay with his Uncle Rayber who has reacted so violently against the fideism of his own brutalized youth that he has become a hardened and hard-hearted atheist. The boy, caught between two equally erroneous philosophies, struggles to find his own way to "truth" without any rational coordinates with which to orient himself. Not surprisingly, he is hopelessly lost in a world in which equally nonsensical influences battle for supremacy.

The brilliance of the novel is not, however, to be found in the battle between irrational faith and equally irrational "rationalism" but in the powerful presence of the idiot child, the son of Uncle Rayber, who probably has Down syndrome. The idiot's name is Bishop, which was presumably selected by O'Connor with an ironic symbolism in mind, "bishop" deriving etymologically from the Greek *episkopos*, meaning "above-looking" or, more prosaically, "overseer." Like the other characters, Bishop is not rational, though in his case the absence of reason is not due to the arrogance of ignorance but to a physical handicap, and yet his very existence serves to illustrate the presence of unequivocal love in the gloom of the grotesque. Since, symbolically (and even, ultimately, literally) the presence of unequivocal love serves as the presence of Christ, the Overseer, it is in the holy fool that we see the Holy Innocence which makes sense of the darkness of sin and ultimately vanquishes it. The novel would be meaningless, a postmodern nightmare, without the presence of such love, which is nothing less than Meaning Itself. It is, therefore, hardly surprising that the equally irrational Tarwater and Rayber can see no point or purpose in Bishop's life or existence, seeing him as subhuman.

For anyone blessed to know someone with Down syndrome, the most excruciating experience in reading the novel will be the way in which Bishop, this holy fool, this holy innocent, is treated with such disdain and cruelty. To see this sweet and simple lamb of innocence abused so brutally by those who are shackled and blinded by their pride and prejudice is almost insufferable. And yet the suffering of the innocent one has to be suffered, in both senses of the word. It has to be felt as pain and permitted for the necessary lesson it teaches.

And what is the lesson that Flannery O'Connor teaches? It is the same lesson that the life and presence of those with Down syndrome teach us. It is that love is inseparable from suffering. It is inseparable from the self-sacrifice demanded in laying down our lives for the beloved. It has been said that most of us are here to learn but that some of us are here to teach and that those with Down syndrome and similar disabilities, such as O'Connor's character Bishop, are the ones who are here to teach. This, I believe, is the deepest lesson that Flannery O'Connor teaches in this most violent and brilliant of novels.

24

C. S. Lewis and J. R. R. Tolkien

We conclude our panoramic overview of the literature that every Catholic should know with two of the most popular writers of all time, C. S. Lewis and J. R. R. Tolkien. In any list of all-time bestsellers, the names of Tolkien and Lewis figure prominently. *The Lion, the Witch and the Wardrobe* by Lewis and *The Lord of the Rings* and *The Hobbit* by Tolkien have recorded global sales which only a handful of other books can match. Their success is nothing less than phenomenal.

Those wishing to understand the Christian philosophy of storytelling that underpins the work of these two great writers, who were also great friends, should read Tolkien's essay "On Fairy Stories," his poem "Mythopoeia," and his allegorical short story "Leaf by Niggle," all of which were published together in a single volume, *Tree and Leaf.*

C. S. LEWIS

C. S. Lewis was a man of letters who wrote in many different literary genres. Apart from his most influential work, *Mere Christianity*, he wrote several other important works of non-fiction, most notably *Miracles*, in which he makes a convincing philosophical case for the intervention of the supernatural in the natural order. He is, however, best known for his fictional works, most especially perhaps for *The Chronicles of Narnia*, a series of seven novels written for children. Although ostensibly for a younger readership, the Narnian Chronicles are so full of profound theological and philosophical insights that they offer spiritual and intellectual nourishment to readers of all ages. In particular, the climax to *The Last Battle*, the final book in the series, contains some of the finest eschatological theology in the English language. It is indeed a proof of Lewis's genius that he can embed such mystical profundity within the text and context of a children's story.

Lewis's earliest sortie into fiction was *The Pilgrim's Regress*, a formal allegory which is a largely autobiographical account of Lewis's own conversion from atheism to Christianity. Journeying from his childhood home in Puritania, representing the puritanical Calvinism that Lewis experienced as a child in Northern Ireland, the protagonist, "John," meets various personified abstractions, representing the ideas Lewis encountered in his journey towards conversion, including the spirits of the Enlightenment and of Romanticism, and the Spirit of the Age, the last of which is overthrown by Reason, personified as a beautiful maiden on a horse. Eventually, and reluctantly, John submits to Mother Kirk (Mother Church) and is baptized.

If *The Pilgrim's Regress* was obviously modelled after its progenitor, John Bunyan's *The Pilgrim's Progress*, a seventeenth-century formal allegory, *The Great Divorce* owes an obvious debt to Dante's *Inferno* in its exploration of the psychology of the damned. As we meet the various doomed souls, each of whom rejects the love of God and the grace being offered, it becomes evident that God does not condemn anyone to Hell. Those in Hell freely choose to go there, preferring the alienated Self to the Communion of Love. The same masterful understanding of the human psyche is present in *The Screwtape Letters*, in which

Lewis plays devil's advocate in order to expose the diabolical nature of sin.

The Space Trilogy, sometimes also known as the Cosmic Trilogy or the Ransom Trilogy, is a series of science fiction novels in which Lewis counters the progressivism and scientism of the previous generation of science fiction writers, such as H. G. Wells. In *Out of the Silent Planet*, the first of the series, Lewis deploys the character of Elwin Ransom, a middle-aged philologist modelled on Lewis's friend J. R. R. Tolkien, to counter the ideas of Dr. Weston, a mad physicist modelled in part on the anthropocentric humanism of Wells and his ilk. Having been kidnapped by Weston and his accomplice Dick Devine, Ransom is taken to Malacandra (Mars), where the three men meet various strange beings, most notably the angelic eldila, whose wisdom exposes the shallow and narrowly bigoted nature of Weston's philosophical materialism.

In the second book of the Trilogy, *Perelandra*, the action takes place on Venus to which Ransom has been sent to counter the designs of the Black Oyarsa of Thulcandra (Satan). He once again encounters his old enemy Dr. Weston, whose presence on the planet threatens the primal and unfallen innocence of the Lady, whom Ransom has been sent to protect. The novel then revolves around the dialectical engagement between Ransom and Weston, the former arguing for a traditional Christian understanding of the cosmos and the latter for an arrogant materialism that is eventually exposed as being satanic in its origin and purpose.

In the final book of the Trilogy, *That Hideous Strength*, Ransom, who is now older and has become something of a mystic, is the voice of sanity and sanctity in a world darkened by the forces of materialism. Set against the backdrop of an England in the grips of scientism, the novel is kaleidoscopic in its mixing of seemingly incompatible literary genres. Ostensibly a science fiction story, it incorporates an Arthurian dimension in the presence of the resurrected Merlin and presents a plethora of modern ideologies and philosophies in an unholy alliance against the forces of goodness and truth.

Lewis's final work of fiction, and the one that he believed was his best, is *Till We Have Faces*, a retelling of the ancient myth of Cupid and Psyche from Apuleius's *Metamorphoses*. This is much more subtle than Lewis's other fiction in its handling of the allegorical dimension, leaving many of Lewis's admirers confused by its apparent obliqueness. At root, the novel is an exploration of the nature of faith, particularly from the perspective of one who lacks it. Lewis makes Psyche's palace invisible to mortal eyes and thereby presents a challenge to those who cannot see it. The way in which Orual, the protagonist, responds to this hidden reality provides the dynamism of the plot.

In his fiction, Lewis sought to engage with the intellectual currents of the modern age in order to highlight the fallacious nature of modernity's view of reality and to show the perennial and prevailing wisdom of Christianity. His voyages to other planets and to the gloomy world of the afterlife are intended to awaken us from the nightmare of nihilism so that we can rise from our bed of sleep to the dawning of the miraculous day that God has given us.

J. R. R. TOLKIEN

The Hobbit

The Hobbit is much more than simply a children's story. At its deepest level of meaning, and great children's literature always has a deep level of meaning, *The Hobbit* is a pilgrimage of grace, in which its protagonist, Bilbo Baggins, becomes grown-up in the most important sense, which is the growth in wisdom and virtue. Throughout the course of his adventure—and every pilgrimage is an adventure—the hobbit develops the habit of virtue and grows in sanctity. Thus *The Hobbit* illustrates the priceless truth that we only become wise men (*homo sapiens*) when we realize that we are pilgrims on a purposeful journey through life (*homo viator*).

Apart from the story's status as a Christian bildungsroman, charting Bilbo's rite of passage from ignorance to wisdom and from bourgeois vice to heroic virtue, *The Hobbit* parallels *The Lord of the Rings* in the mystical suggestiveness of its treatment of Divine Providence and serves as a moral commentary on the words of Christ that "where your treasure is, there will your heart be also" (Matthew 6:21). In this context, Bilbo's journey from the homely comfort of the Shire to the uncomfortable lessons learned on the Lonely Mountain, in parallel with Frodo's journey from the Shire to Mount Doom, is a mirror of Everyman's journey through life. It is in this sense that Tolkien wrote in his celebrated and cerebral essay "On Fairy Stories" that "the fairy-story ... may be used as a Mirour de l'Omme" or as "the Mirror of scorn and pity towards Man." In short, we are meant to see ourselves reflected in the character of Bilbo Baggins and our lives reflected in his journey from the Shire to the Lonely Mountain. For the Christian, who spurns the nihilism of the existentialist, life is charged with meaning and purpose and is at the service of the final goal and purpose of every life, which is to be united with the Divine Life of God in Heaven. This being so, every life is a quest to achieve the goal of Heaven and everyone is called to grow in virtue so that he may attain sanctity, and have the power, through grace, to overcome the monsters and demons which seek to prevent him achieving his goal. It is in this way that we are meant to read *The Hobbit*, and it is in this way, and this way alone, that we find its deepest and most applicable meaning.

In truth, Bilbo Baggins bears a remarkable resemblance to each of us, his diminutive size and furry feet notwithstanding.

He seeks the respectable life of bourgeois gentility. He likes tea and toast, and jam and pickles; he has wardrobes full of clothes and lots of pantries full of food. He is a creature of comfort dedicated to the creature comforts. Nothing could be further from Bilbo Baggins's mind, or further from his desire, than the prospect, or the threat, of an adventure. He is dedicated to the easy life and would find the prospect of taking up his cross and following the heroic path of self-sacrifice utterly anathema. The unexpected party at the beginning of the story, in which the daily habits of the hobbit are disrupted by the arrival of unexpected and unwelcome guests is, therefore, a necessary disruption. It is the intervention into his cosy life of an element of inconvenience or suffering that serves as a wake-up call and a call to action. Gandalf introduces the reluctant Bilbo to Thorin Oakenshield and the other dwarves in order to prompt him into an adventure, the purpose of which is ostensibly the recovery of the dwarves' treasure but also, on the moral level at which the story works, the growth in wisdom and virtue, through suffering and sacrifice, of Bilbo himself. In losing his bourgeois respectability, the price he must pay for becoming an adventurer, he forsakes the world and the worldly in favour of the pearl of great price.

The irony is that Bilbo's position at the outset of the story is an ironic and symbolic prefiguring of Smaug's surrounding himself with treasure in his "home" in the Lonely Mountain. Bilbo, on a microcosmic scale, is, therefore, nothing less than a figure and prefigurement of Smaug. He is afflicted with the dragon sickness. His pilgrimage to the Lonely Mountain is the means by which he will be cured of this materialist malady. It is a *via dolorosa*, a path of suffering, the following of which will heal him of his self-centredness and teach him to give himself self-sacrificially to others.

The paradoxical consequence of the dragon sickness is that the things possessed possess the possessor. Thus Bilbo is a slave to his possessions at the beginning of the story and is liberated from them, or from his addiction to them, by its end. Similarly, Smaug is a prisoner of his own treasure-hoard, unable to leave his brooding over his possessions for fear that someone might steal something. The dragon's sickness is especially ironic because it is obvious that Smaug has no practical use for any of the treasure. He is a slave of something that is essentially useless to him. His dragon-heart is possessed by the addiction to something which, for a dragon, is nothing but trivia and trash.

As the unfolding of the plot reveals, dragon sickness is not restricted to dragons. Apart from Bilbo's own affliction with it, the dwarves are clearly driven by their desire to regain the treasure and Thorin becomes utterly possessed by his obsession with hoarding it for himself once the dragon is slain. His heart is poisoned by his possessive gold-lust and he forgets his friendship with Bilbo, and the debt that he owes to him, in the hardness and blindness that the dragon sickness causes. His reconciliation with Bilbo after he is mortally wounded in the Battle of Five Armies signifies his recovery from the dragon sickness. His final words to Bilbo, uttered with his dying breath, encapsulate one of the chief morals of the work: "If more of us valued food and cheer and song above hoarded gold, it would be a merrier world."

Bilbo's recovery from the dragon sickness is signified by his giving away of the Arkenstone and any further claim upon his share of the treasure as a means of healing the rift between the warring parties. When Gandalf proclaims at the story's end that Bilbo is no longer the hobbit that he was, we know that he is changed for the better. He no longer places his heart at the service of his worldly possessions but seeks instead those treasures of the heart to be found in wisdom and virtue. He is healed and he is whole, or, as Tolkien the Catholic might say, he is whole because he is holy. The hobbit had attained the habit of virtue and, as befits the hero of any good fairy story, he now knew what was necessary to live happily ever after.

The Lord of the Rings

Tolkien stated on December 2, 1953, that "*The Lord of the Rings* is of course a fundamentally religious and Catholic work; unconsciously so at first, but consciously in the revision."[1] Five years later, on October 25, 1958, he discussed the existence of a "scale of significance" appertaining to the relationship between himself and his work. At the very top of this scale of significance, as the single-most important of the "really significant" elements, was the fact that "I am a Christian (which can be deduced from my stories), and in fact a Roman Catholic."[2] According to Tolkien's friend George Sayer, "*The Lord of the Rings* would have been very different if Tolkien hadn't been a Christian. He thought it a profoundly Christian book."[3] Since, however, and as Tolkien explained, "the religious element is absorbed into the story and the symbolism,"[4] the accurate discernment of the presence of this "absorbed" religious element is necessary for anyone seeking an understanding of the deeper meaning of *The Lord of the Rings*.

The centrality of the hidden presence of Christ is discernible most insistently in the date that Tolkien ascribes to the destruction of the Ring. Gandalf tells Samwise Gamgee that "the New Year will always now begin upon the twenty-fifth of March when Sauron fell." Elsewhere, in one of the appendices to *The Lord of the Rings*, March 25 is given as "the date of the downfall of the Barad-dûr," and the New Year is said to begin on March 25, "in commemoration of the fall of Sauron

---

1   Humphrey Carpenter, ed., *The Letters of J. R. R. Tolkien* (London: George Allen & Unwin, 1981), 172.

2   Ibid., 288.

3   George Sayer, interview with Joseph Pearce, September 3, 1997.

4   Carpenter, ed., *The Letters of J. R. R. Tolkien*, 172.

and the deeds of the Ring-bearers." This date is of singular significance in the Christian calendar. It is the Feast of the Annunciation, the date on which Christians celebrate the Incarnation of Christ, the Word becoming Flesh in the womb of the Blessed Virgin. It is also traditionally believed to be the date on which Christ's Crucifixion occurred. Annunciation Day, as it was called, was also the start of the New Year in many countries in Christian Europe during the Middle Ages.

The theological connection between the Incarnation and the Crucifixion, and hence the logical assumption that the two events happened on the same significant date, is that both events were necessary for the Redemption of Man from Original Sin. Put simply, Christians believe that Original Sin was "unmade" by the Life, Death and Resurrection of Christ. Original Sin is "the One Sin to rule them all and in the darkness bind them," as the ring in *The Lord of the Rings* is "the One Ring to rule them all . . . and in the darkness bind them." The One Ring and the One Sin are symbolic similitudes. As the One Ring is "unmade" on Mount Doom so the One Sin is "unmade" on the hill of Golgotha, the place of the skull.

March 25 is, therefore, the key that unlocks the deepest meaning of *The Lord of the Rings*. If the Ring is synonymous with sin in general and Original Sin in particular, the Christocentric aspects of the work become apparent. Frodo, as the Ring-Bearer, emerges as a Christ figure, the one who bears the Cross, and with it the sins and the hopes of humanity. He emerges also as an Everyman figure, in the tradition of the mediaeval Mystery Plays, who takes up his own cross in emulation of Christ. His journey through Mordor (Death) to the summit of Mount Doom (Golgotha/Death) is thus a reminder both of Christ's archetypal *via dolorosa* and also of the path of sorrows that Everyman is called to follow in the quest for sanctity and salvation. This subliminal dialectic is signified still further by Frodo's departure from Rivendell on December 25, connecting Frodo's journey to the life of Christ, from birth to death.

Although Frodo emerges as the most obvious Christ figure, it should be remembered that Tolkien disliked formal or crude allegory. As such, Frodo is only a Christ figure insofar as he is the Ring-Bearer, and insofar as the Ring can be seen to signify Sin. In every other respect he is simply a hobbit of the Shire. He is not a figure of Christ at all times in the way that a character in a formal allegory is merely a personified abstraction of the thing or person he represents, such as, for example, the character of "Reason" in C. S. Lewis's *The Pilgrim's Regress*. In this context it is important to recall Tolkien's distinction between the formal allegory he despised and the allegorical *applicability* he espoused. According to Tolkien's understanding of applicability, aspects of a story can be applicable to the world beyond the story, most notably to the world inhabited by the reader.

With regard to Christological applicability, it can be seen that other characters in the story, besides Frodo, emerge as Christ figures at certain *applicable* moments. Gandalf reminds us of Christ in his "death," "resurrection," and "transfiguration," especially in the way that Tolkien's description of Gandalf's "resurrection" resonates unmistakably with the Gospel accounts of Christ's Transfiguration. Aragorn's descent to the Paths of the Dead reminds us of Christ's descent into Hell following the Crucifixion. Aragorn, like Christ, is "King of the Dead" who has the power to set the suffering souls free of the death-curse. Similarly, Aragorn is a Christ figure in his role as healer. As Ioreth, wise-woman of Gondor, proclaimed: "The hands of the king are the hands of a healer, and so shall the rightful king be known."

For Tolkien, as he insisted so memorably in his famous conversation with C. S. Lewis on the nature of mythology in September 1931, Christianity was the "True Myth," the myth that really happened, the myth that gives ultimate meaning to all the lesser myths. Similarly, the Person of Christ is the True Hero who gives ultimate meaning to the heroism of all the lesser heroes. It is no surprise, therefore, that Tolkien's heroes emerge as Christ figures, reminding his readers of the archetypal Hero who gives his own lesser heroes their meaning and their very *raison d'être*.

If there is one major lesson that we can learn from the example of Tolkien and Lewis, then it is that Christian authors can influence and impact the modern world with the beauty and profundity of their art. May their example guide us as we journey forth armed with the great works of literature to evangelize our own age with the timeless power of all that is good and true and beautiful.

47
authors

25

Great Works of Literature
Every Catholic Should Know

We will conclude our survey of what every Catholic should know about literature with a selection of 100 great works of literature that every Catholic should aspire to read.

1. *The Iliad* by Homer
2. *The Odyssey* by Homer
3. *Antigone* by Sophocles
4. *Oedipus Rex* by Sophocles
5. *Oedipus at Colonus* by Sophocles
6. *The Aeneid* by Virgil
7. *The Consolation of Philosophy* by Boethius
8. *Beowulf* (Anonymous)
9. *The Divine Comedy* by Dante
10. *The Canterbury Tales* by Geoffrey Chaucer
11. *Utopia* by Thomas More
12. *Collected Poems* by Robert Southwell
13. *Richard III* by William Shakespeare
14. *Romeo and Juliet* by William Shakespeare
15. *The Merchant of Venice* by William Shakespeare
16. *The Merry Wives of Windsor* by William Shakespeare
17. *Julius Caesar* by William Shakespeare
18. *Hamlet* by William Shakespeare
19. *Twelfth Night* by William Shakespeare

20. *Measure for Measure* by William Shakespeare
21. *Othello* by William Shakespeare
22. *King Lear* by William Shakespeare
23. *Macbeth* by William Shakespeare
24. *The Winter's Tale* by William Shakespeare
25. *The Tempest* by William Shakespeare
26. *Don Quixote* by Miguel de Cervantes
27. *The Metaphysical Poets* (Penguin Classics edition)
28. *Paradise Lost* by John Milton
29. *The Hind and the Panther* by John Dryden
30. *Gulliver's Travels* by Jonathan Swift
31. *Romantic Poets: Blake, Wordsworth, and Coleridge* (Ignatius Critical Edition)
32. *Sense and Sensibility* by Jane Austen
33. *Pride and Prejudice* by Jane Austen
34. *Mansfield Park* by Jane Austen
35. *Emma* by Jane Austen
36. *Persuasion* by Jane Austen
37. *Northanger Abbey* by Jane Austen
38. *Frankenstein* by Mary Shelley
39. *The Betrothed* by Alessandro Manzoni
40. *Wuthering Heights* by Emily Brontë
41. *Jane Eyre* by Charlotte Brontë
42. *Evangeline* by Henry Wadsworth Longfellow
43. *A Christmas Carol* by Charles Dickens
44. *A Tale of Two Cities* by Charles Dickens
45. *Great Expectations* by Charles Dickens
46. *David Copperfield* by Charles Dickens
47. *Loss and Gain* by John Henry Newman
48. *Callista* by John Henry Newman
49. *Poems* by Gerard Manley Hopkins
50. *War and Peace* by Leo Tolstoy
51. *Anna Karenina* by Leo Tolstoy
52. *The Idiot* by Fyodor Dostoyevsky

87. *Out of the Silent Planet* by C. S. Lewis
88. *Perelandra* by C. S. Lewis
89. *That Hideous Strength* by C. S. Lewis
90. *Till We Have Faces* by C. S. Lewis
91. *The Chronicles of Narnia* by C. S. Lewis
92. *The Complete Stories* by Flannery O'Connor
93. *Wise Blood* by Flannery O'Connor
94. *The Violent Bear It Away* by Flannery O'Connor
95. *A Man for All Seasons* by Robert Bolt
96. *One Day in the Life of Ivan Denisovich* by Aleksandr Solzhenitsyn
97. *Cancer Ward* by Aleksandr Solzhenitsyn
98. *First Circle* by Aleksandr Solzhenitsyn
99. *Love in the Ruins* by Walker Percy
100. *Lancelot* by Walker Percy